LIVING WITH
WILDFIRE

ALSO BY MAUREEN GILMER:

The Colorful Dry Garden
Palm Springs Style Gardening
Vegetable Gardening in Desert, Drought and Dry Times
Gaining Ground
Water Works
The Complete Guide to Northern California Gardening
The Complete Guide to Southern California Gardening
Living on Flood Plains and Wetlands
California Wildfire Landscaping
Easy Lawn and Garden Care
Redwoods and Roses

LIVING WITH
WILDFIRE
A HOMEOWNER'S HANDBOOK

MAUREEN GILMER

GUILFORD, CONNECTICUT

An imprint of The Rowman & Littlefield Publishing Group, Inc.
4501 Forbes Blvd., Ste. 200
Lanham, MD 20706
www.rowman.com

Distributed by NATIONAL BOOK NETWORK

British Library Cataloguing in Publication Information available

Library of Congress Cataloging-in-Publication Data available

ISBN 978-1-4930-3836-7 (paperback)
ISBN 978-1-4930-3837-4 (e-book)

♾™ The paper used in this publication meets the minimum requirements of American National Standard for Information Sciences—Permanence of Paper for Printed Library Materials, ANSI/NISO Z39.48-1992.

*For my cousin, Michael Esnard, who believed in the Fire
Safe Councils and was instrumental in helping his town of
Idyllwild survive the horrible July 2018 fire, proving they
achieved an excellent national model of local cooperation.*

*And the thousands of men and women who each year
willingly face the fire line battling these ever greater
and more dangerous wildfires.*

CONTENTS

PREFACE

By the time this book goes to press there is no doubt that another summer of equally devastating fires will have charred many of our most scenic wildlands. It's August and the skies are hazy with smoke from enormous fires burning simultaneously in British Columbia, Washington, Idaho, Montana, Colorado, Oregon, and California. There is a somber pall cast over the west because most of these fires were so large they became impossible to control. Many will burn until the first rain or snow of autumn.

Many communities saw for the first time the awesome power of fire as it moves through fuel-rich forests, some of which have not burned for a century or longer. Since we began fire suppression, the population of the West's most volatile forest land has grown, and thin fingers of development extend further and further in to these decadent fuel-rich stands. People ask why this year, and why the fires are so vicious, the answer is simple: fire suppression and increased residential development.

What this means to those who live in fire-prone areas is that wildfires cannot be as easily controlled as in the past. Each year more homes are built in rural forested lands in either dense communities or widely scattered homes and cabins. As the fires indeed become more aggressive, the complication of fighting them in and around residential areas is an enormous challenge to firefighters. In addition, parts of some Western states have no protection, or only minimal firefighting facilities. New residents moving from the East or out of California are discovering too late that their new homes in the woods are unprotected, highly vulnerable, and facing some of the worst fire conditions of the twentieth century and the twenty-first.

Few homeowners stop to consider the dilemma facing the firefighters of the West. For each home in the path of the fire, more men and women must pull off the fire line to protect the house. When many houses are in the area, the manpower is further diluted, and officers must make snap decisions on whether to defend a house or let it burn in order to keep more people working on the fire line.

As residents in fire-prone ecosystems, it is every homeowner's duty to make firefighting easier and more effective. Irresponsible behavior such as failing to manage vegetation, building with attractive but highly flammable materials, and poorly maintained access roads complicate firefighting, and may ultimately lead to death. We can no longer turn away from our responsibility to make our homes as firefighter-friendly as we can. People are dying.

This book is designed to provide residents with the information they need to make a home less vulnerable to fire. It details how to use water and other means to protect a home in the face of an oncoming wildfire. Not only does this increase the chances of a home's survival, it also ensures there is a maximum number of trained people on the fire line, which is essential if the fire is to be stopped at all.

ACKNOWLEDGMENTS

Special thanks to those who were so helpful in supplying the facts and valuable information required to write this book. Their encouragement is much appreciated.

Ernst D. Paschke, District Conservationist, USDA Soil Conservation Service

Dan Smith, Director of Communications, American Forests

Gerald Adams, Fire Marshall, Battalion Chief, North Lake Tahoe Fire Protection District

Tim Paysen, Riverside Forest Fire Lab

Steve Arno, Intermountain Research Station, Montana

Steve Kroeger, Division Chief, California Department of Forestry and Fire Protection, Oroville

Steve Carroll, Public Affairs Officer, Boise National Forest

Jason M. Greenlee, Executive Director, International Association of Wildland Fire

Bruce Turbeville, Fire Prevention Education Specialist, California Department of Forestry and Fire Prevention

INTRODUCTION

The western inland forests that we so love and cherish for what they do for the environment, for the economy, and especially for our souls have, for the past 100 years, been experiencing dramatic and unhealthy changes. The primary cause of this major, region-wide problem has been the exclusion of fire from the forests.

R. NEIL SAMPSON
AMERICAN FORESTS

T he forests of the Western states depend on fire as a thinning, renewing mechanism. Fires were naturally ignited by lightning, but also spread by Native Americans who helped fire do its job in ecosystems from coast to coast. They knew the fires encouraged a crop of nutritious grasses for wildlife, kept the land open for travel and hunting, and renewed some fire-dependent species. Fires during the pre-European times were slower moving and burned at lower temperatures for a much shorter time. They were healthy for our forests.

With settlement, fire suppression was important to protect farms, towns, mills, and mining camps. It began nearly a century ago, and in the last fifty years has been very successful. This interrupted the natural burn cycle and thus altered the natural balance of vegetation and fuels. Fire suppression combined with the results of early logging have created an artificial condition where there is no mechanism to discourage the sprouting and growth of every seedling. This has produced a population explosion in the forests, which were once open and parklike, as described by early pioneers. Try to walk through much of our forest ecosystems today and you'll encounter an impenetrable thicket of vegetation not at all similar to these early reports.

To put this into a statistical form, studies of ponderosa pine forests in Arizona are similar to others in many of the Western states. The Arizona study proves that historic density of trees ranged from 25 to 60 per acre. Today we are seeing densities well over 275 per acre, which means the competition for limited light, water, and soil nutrients is keen. This is even more important in the West where drought is not uncommon, and under normal circumstances trees can survive these dry periods. But today's vegetation-choked forests can no longer stand up to drought, and the vast majority of standing dead trees we see is often caused by insects which may only enter the tree when it is suffering dehydration.

Comparative photography has become a valuable tool in determining how forests change over time. This 1895 photograph shows how arid forests of the inland West appeared to the early settlers. Periodic fires were responsible for maintaining such a condition. Trees are widely spaced and predominantly pines well adapted to extremes of temperature and periodic drought.
COURTESY OF UNIVERSITY OF MONTANA

Such highly stressed forest lands are vulnerable to wildfire. There is more standing dead timber, a thicker carpet of forest litter, and the greater number of seedlings and saplings clustered beneath the large old trees. This spells a recipe for disaster. Trees which have stood through centuries of cleansing fires are now the victims of intense bonfires beneath their canopies when this material combines with an abundance of dead trees to burn hotter than ever before. No tree can survive these new fires, not even a redwood.

Today forest experts are preaching a new dogma. No longer can we view all fires as bad because history tells us they were beneficial in the past. Today many believe fire can restore forest health, but not until we

The same homesite eighty-five years later. It bears little resemblance to the earlier view and shows a landscape ripe for a serious fire sure to kill all the trees. This stand of timber is no longer pine, but predominately Douglas fir. When fires ceased at the turn of the century, the faster growing Douglas fir began filling in the gaps between pines to ultimately crowd them out altogether. This landscape reflects the current condition of our forests throughout most of the West.
COURTESY OF UNIVERSITY OF MONTANA

American Forests, a national conservation organization, is deeply concerned with forest health in the West. They have identified the critical states where national forests are suffering due to overcrowding and fire suppression. Though most people don't live in these recognized wilderness areas, similar conditions are growing in wild/ands throughout these states and many others.

Alaska Three million acres of spruce forests are under attack from the spruce budworm, which has spread rapidly during the last five years.

Arizona In the San Francisco peaks, over 300,000 acres of mixed conifer forests are being devastated by the spruce budworm and bark beetles.

California This state has always suffered serious fires due to Gold Rush-era logging and fire suppression. Today the Modoc National Forest is battling drought and pests.

Idaho Boise and Payette national forests are suffering beetle damage, drought, and disease, fueling some of the most serious fires ever seen on those watersheds.

Nevada In the Lake Tahoe Basin, firs have replaced the ponderosa and Jeffrey pines, a severe alteration that has caused as much as a third of the forest to die out.

Oregon The Blue Mountains and much of this state have been so altered that the forests are no longer self-sustaining. As populations grow here more homes will be at risk.

Washington Spruce budworm, bark beetle, and other diseases are causing serious problems in the Colville, Wenatchee, and Okanogan national forests.

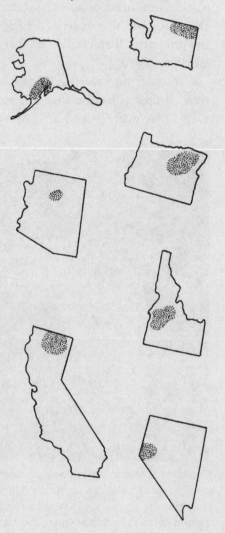

manually thin the undergrowth to keep fire temperatures to a level that will not harm the older trees. Some activists cry "let it burn" because they understand only half of the equation. But these people fail to realize that we cannot burn such fuel-rich forests all at once or nothing would be left to reforest the land.

As each fire season approaches experts are becoming uneasy about the future. They know that declining forest health is occurring on such a massive scale there is too little time to thin the trees and start control burning action. This is partly due to shrinking budgets, and partly because environmental regulation has limited the options. Yet many hope that a combined effort between the federal government, state government, and private industry can find the solutions which will save our forests. In the meantime, residents in fire-prone areas must become aware of the critical situation and how they fit into the big picture. Because the wheels of government turn slowly, and as policymakers in Washington fiddle away like Nero over emotional environmental issues—Rome is burning.

1

HOW VEGETATION AND TOPOGRAPHY INFLUENCE WILDFIRES

Much of the United States has experienced an increase in population since World War II and is expected to continue growing at a similar rate. This stimulates a continual need for new housing. The most desirable areas are developed first, then growth must reach for new sites in more rural, steep terrain. This difficult access combined with various types of native vegetation creates a volatile situation that threatens many communities from coast to coast. The urban-wildland interface or "I Zone" is a new term being used by today's fire suppression and land management experts. It describes the increasing number of situations where residential development contacts natural wildland ecosystems.

Firefighting experts would like to see more stringent controls on where development occurs in order to reduce situations that are in no way defensible, such as homes on steep hillsides where access is limited. They lament insufficient building codes concerning architecture, building materials, landscaping, and management of native vegetation. Some communities have legislated more stringent fire safety regulations that demand only the most basic vegetation controls, such as clearing fuels around homes and chimney caps. But this is just a small step, and with wildland fuels accumulating, we need to take giant leaps in establishing regulations to protect homesites.

THE NATURE OF THE BEAST

All wildfires are not the same. The behavior of a fire is described by factors such as temperature, duration, and speed of travel. Each of these is influenced by the lay of the land, or topography, and the amount of vegetation, or fuel. When evaluating a homesite in terms of wildfire vulnerability, the area outside the yard or property lines is critical. This is because wildfires typically originate off site and must travel to your home, unlike a house fire, which starts within the home itself. For example, your homesite may be protected by well-designed and maintained firescape—a defensible space landscape. But if your next-door neighbor's house is crowded by tall weeds and overgrown brush, or if your property backs up to dense, unmanaged native vegetation, the heat and ash generated may still threaten your safety. This illustrates how important it is for entire communities to work together in reducing fire danger.

The finest example of this community effort was achieved by Neighbors for Defensible Space in the Lake Tahoe Basin, California. Here pine beetles and other factors have created a tremendous amount of standing dead timber. In addition, the original trees in this basin were drought-tolerant ponderosa and Jeffrey pine, which were logged off during the late 1800s. Only the white fir that clustered in cooler spots remained to reforest the area. Today the basin is filled with fir, which are not at all drought tolerant. This illustrates how the types of trees as well as their density has changed.

Citizens of Incline Village, Nevada, led by Fire Marshall Jerry Adams, realized their vulnerability. They organized a group that developed a comprehensive program of local forest management and the creation of "defensible space" around homesites. It has been highly successful and became the model for many other groups acting to reduce the overall fire danger in their communities, including those in suburban Colorado and Oregon where fire danger is at an all-time high.

Keep in mind this is no simple matter. "Neighbors" had to coordinate input, demands, and concerns from many different agencies not always agreement with each other. It was a long and arduous effort working with the US Forest Service, Tahoe Regional Planning Agency, Nevada

HABITAT AND YOU

Firefighting agencies are responsible for protecting residential areas from the threat of wildfires. Historically they have reduced the threat by controlling vegetation through prescribed burning where the terrain and access made this a safe solution. They also have used goat herds to consume vegetation. Some rural homeowners in rolling grasslands disk the soil around their houses each year in order to turn under the dry grass before fire season.

In the last two decades, the Endangered Species Act has identified various plants and animals that are threatened with extinction due to a shrinking habitat. This program dictated that certain areas in which these species live should be preserved at any cost by simply leaving the sites untouched. As a result, efforts to burn, graze, or disk away the fire hazard have been hampered or curtailed entirely by law.

The reality of this approach to land management is that the species may be at greater risk due to such neglect. For example, prescribed burns allow wildlife to move into other areas outside the fire zone. Eventually they will return with the vegetation. If left untouched, this same area will burn far hotter and over such a large, uncontrolled area that the wildlife cannot escape, and plants that normally survive natural burns, such as mature ponderosa pine, will be permanently damaged or killed. Today in the Boise National Forest, rare trout species are being "poached in their streams," a scenario rarely encountered until recent years.

A new example of this in the state of Virginia came to the attention of the Nature Conservancy. The Peter's mountain mallow, a perennial

Division of Forestry, as well as other environmental groups. Yet all were in agreement: the dense predominately fir forests were sure to decline from invasions of pests and disease, then burn in cataclysmic fires. Also supporting the project were the North Lake Tahoe Chamber of Commerce, University of Nevada at Reno Cooperative Extension, and the North Lake Tahoe Fire District.

There are some other important terms to know which relate to the types of fuels that feed a fire.

wildflower, was discovered in 1927, and a group of fifty plants were the only known individuals. By 1991 only four remained. Concerned, the Nature Conservancy, Virginia Tech, and the state took action to save them. Tree rings showed an historic pattern of recurring fire for that forest, and lab tests revealed that the mallow seeds germinated far more readily after exposure to fire. Fire also reduced competition from surrounding plants with seedlings more vigorous and greedy than the mallow.

In May 1992, foresters burned a test area where the mallow once grew and afterward the first year new seedlings were found. The following year they conducted a second burn and about five hundred seeds germinated. Conservancy president John Sawhill stated the new attitude toward fire and wildlife conservation: "This shows us that simply setting aside land to protect rare or endangered species does not necessarily guarantee their protection. The remarkable comeback of Peter's Mountain mallow through the use of prescribed burning demonstrates the important role that this type of land management tool plays."

Studies are now proving that a better way to preserve endangered species is to actively thin and burn areas where vegetation has become so overgrown. This opens up the land for predatory species and encourages a more prolific food supply. There is bound to be enormous controversy in the future over active versus passive habitat preservation, and within this dilemma resides the residential homeowner. But there is hope that continual efforts by both firefighting agencies and citizens will ultimately influence the hard line environmentalists who tend to cling to their belief that an untouched habitat is the best habitat.

AERIAL FUELS These consist of parts of plants located over 5 feet above the ground, typically the canopies of trees and tops of taller shrubs. Crown fires feed upon aerial fuels and travel quickly through tree tops. If they contact shrubs or dead trees with low branches, these bring the flames downward to the ground.

URBAN FUELS This is a new concept that is based on fire behavior in cities. Sometimes the source is a house fire, but it can also originate from embers generated by wildland fires a long distance away. In this case rooftops act much like closely spaced trees in a forest. Roofing of closely built homes allows a fire to travel via aerial fuels to ignite great numbers of homes as rapidly as trees in a forest fire and with similar, devastating results. Shade trees in subdivisions act as stepping stones to help fire jump from house to house.

SURFACE FUELS This type of fuel consists of both living and dead portions of plants from the soil level to about four feet high. The material lying on the ground is termed litter, and consists of brush, leaves, twigs, seeds, pods, cones, and in some cases fallen trees. Surface fuels are not just restricted to wildlands. Flames can be fed by piles of lumber, household garbage, garden prunings, mounds of leaves, chaff from string trimmers, and even wood decks.

GROUND FUELS Ground fires are fed by fuels beneath the surface litter called duff, which often includes humus or organic matter in the soil. The greatest danger of ground fires is that they can smolder for weeks because there is insufficient oxygen to create flame. But when conditions

Homes that back up to natural open spaces are the most vulnerable. Should the area be designated as habitat for endangered species, the ability to create a defensible space may be restricted by wildlife agencies responsible for enforcement of the Endangered Species Act.

are right, such as very low humidity or wind, they can flare up without warning. Ground fuel fires are especially dangerous after wildfires because they can linger unseen for long periods, then flare up when least expected.

FIRESTORMS In many of the most devastating fires, the term firestorm was used to describe a certain type of fire behavior. When winds, high temperatures, and speed of fire movement combine under the right conditions, a violent convection occurs. Convection is the upward movement of hot air containing smoke and embers that rises above a fire. Violent convection is this same mechanism occurring at such great intensity the fire can actually generate its own wind. As these winds increase, the fire becomes more unpredictable, with incredible power and high temperatures concentrated in a single area. It is easy to see why firestorm conditions and the phenomenon associated with them have caused so many deaths in recent years.

FIRE AND TOPOGRAPHY

One seasoned firefighter says that fire moves on the land like water—but in reverse. For example, water runs down a slope, but fire tends to move upward. Where water flows down the sides of a canyon to collect at the bottom in a concentrated stream, fire conversely gathers strength in the low parts of a canyon and rages up the sides. Use this water analogy to visualize how fire is likely to behave in the topography around your homesite.

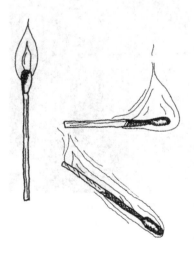

Using a Match to Understand Fire Behavior You can use wood kitchen matches to get a better idea of how fire behaves on sloping ground. Strike the first match and hold it upright as shown and note how long it takes for the flame to reach your fingers. Dispose of the burned match safely. Strike a second match and hold it in a horizontal position to see how this angle increases the speed of the flame. The third match angle downward and you'll discover how rapidly it burns. This third position is the situation of steep slopes with the fuel preheating the vegetation or structures.

Conditions around this fire have caused a firestorm. The heavy black smoke and very tall convection column can exceed 10,000 feet in some cases.

Miraculously, this home escaped damage from the fire that moved up the canyon. Slopes below homes on the left lacked dense vegetation, which clearly slowed the fire and saved them as well.

FIRESCAPING TIP

Experienced firefighters believe that wind often influences fire behavior more than topography. In fire season, dry inland winds are the most serious fire drivers. They also contribute to dreaded firestorms. When reviewing the topography of your homesite or a future homesite, be sure to consider the direction of these winds during the dry fire season for a more accurate picture of vulnerability.

South- and west-facing slopes lend to be more fire prone than those looking north or east. This is because grasses turn brown earlier in the year on these exposures, which extends their fire season. Shrubs and trees also experience greater soil moisture evaporation and higher summer temperatures. Statistics prove that south- and west-facing slopes do experience a higher incidence of fire ignition and burn at greater intensities.

Hot air always travels upward. Fires originating at the base of a slope tend to move quickly upwards because heat is always rising, and on hills this is where unburned fuel is closest to the flames. The steeper the hill, the faster the fire travels. The rising heat actually preheats and dries out the foliage of plants so they ignite far more easily than when fire is moving down slope. If a home is located part way up the hill, it is practically impossible to defend in the blast furnace of rising heat and flame.

"Cliff-hanger" homes perched on the tops of slopes are usually built to take advantage of an unobstructed view. Sometimes portions of the building or attached decking actually jut out from the hill top. These homes are vulnerable in two ways. First, the sheer drop on one or more sides of the building limits access for firefighters. Second, the house sits directly in the path of the flames, and as the fire moves up the slope the rising heat will literally cook the building while bathing it in a rain of embers well before the fire contacts the flammable materials.

These guidelines for fire behavior were fairly predictable in the past until the really big burns of today. Western firefighters have encountered awesome phenomenon fueled by excessively dense timber, a large

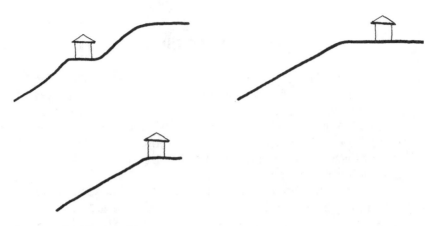

Structure Positions on Slopes

Most homes on steep terrain fit into one of these three scenarios. Upper left: This dangerous, cut-and-fill lot is highly vulnerable, as there is likely to be fuel both above and below the building. There is very little room around the building for defense, and heat radiating off the back slope through windows of the house will ignite interior fuels. Lower left: A house perched on the edge of a hill is pre-heated by the time intense flames reach the top of the slope. There is no space on the slope side of the house for firefighters or their equipment. Right: This house still enjoys a hilltop view but is set back from the top of the slope. This pulls the building out of the direct path of rising heat and flame and provides plenty of room for firefighters to defend the site.

percentage of standing dead trees, and a thick layer of tinder-dry litter on the forest floor. Under such conditions the fire quickly develops its own "weather" that defies topography and becomes unpredictable. It is under these conditions that firefighters are trapped and homeowners have little chance of saving their dwellings. However, if the forest around your community is well managed by thinning and prescribed fire, the chances of such conditions decrease dramatically.

One of the best examples of how you can overcome poor topography with good fire-safe building and landscaping appeared after the Laguna Beach fire in 1993. A single house built in a vulnerable position was left literally unscathed while all the surrounding homes were burned to the ground. It sat perched on the edge of a very steep slope but the owner, both architect and engineer, designed the house with all known fire-resistant qualities. He also planted a fire-resistant green belt around the house. His efforts were so successful that the house has become a landmark, proving the theories of fire-conscious materials and design can sometimes overcome less defensive topography.

A house located on top of the hill but set well back from the edge of a slope is in a better position, but only if it is separated from surrounding vegetation by open space. This breaks the continuity of the fire and creates defensible space, although defense against an intense burn may be virtually hopeless as temperatures and wind reach incredible levels. Fire lines are often drawn on the tops of these ridges to stop flames as they lose momentum before descending the other side of the hill.

Many of our most devastating fires have originated in canyons such as Tanner Gulch in Oregon, Laguna Canyon in California, and Sheep Creek in Idaho. These canyons are narrow, with steep high walls. This arrangement acts much like a chimney, drafting the flames up one or both walls at the same time. In wider canyons the fire may travel up one side,

The number of standing dead trees in this ruin suggests there was once a beautiful, tree-covered homesite. This home had many liabilities: steep terrain for limited access, mid-slope location with fuel both above and below house, and abundance of available conifer fuels.

then jump across to the other side when embers are driven by the wind. A canyon with both walls blazing becomes incredibly hot, with intensity much greater than in any other fire situation.

AMERICA'S MOST FIRE-PRONE ECOSYSTEMS

Fire-prone ecosystems contain large amounts of fuel to feed a wildfire and are typically located in rolling hills or steep mountainous terrain. The greater amount of fuel provided by plants in the ecosystem, the hotter and more aggressive the fire. Most urban-wildland or rural homesites fall

There is much to be learned from the 1993 disaster in Laguna Beach, California. This town, much like those along the Oregon and Washington coast, had only two escape routes, Coast Highway and Laguna Canyon. The fire started in this canyon, developed speed and intensity in this narrow area, and completely blocked evacuation. This forced all traffic to use Coast Highway, which had only one lane in each direction. Fire victims tell of gridlock that prevented escape as flames raged all around them. In many communities such as Malibu, set against steep mountains, major rivers, or other obstructing geographic features, access may be limited to just a few thoroughfares, which must be shared with firefighting trucks and equipment. When traffic jams or gridlock occurs, firefighters cannot reach the fire and residents going the opposite direction cannot escape it. The straw bale rows are designed to catch silt running off these newly burned cliffs to prevent mudslides from inundating the road.

into one of the following defined vegetation types, but in nature there are transition areas where two or more of these blend together. Therefore you must thoroughly understand the type of vegetation surrounding your home because this influences the way you view fire and what must be done reduce the threat.

PRAIRIE GRASSLAND

Grasslands take many forms across our continent, from the sawgrass of the southeastern lowlands to the sod prairie of the Midwest, or the seasonal meadows of the mountains. In the West, grasslands may be entirely open or dotted with oaks, cottonwood, pine, and other native trees. In general, grassland ecosystems are renewed by fire. It burns off the useless chaff to allow sunlight and nutrients to new shoots. Grasslands are typically range pasture for livestock and most are comprised of exotic grasses and broadleaf weeds that have displaced the natives.

Homes and farms are common sights in prairie grasslands. This example shows that grasslands may be surrounded by very dry hill country, and by late summer these meadows will be tinder dry. Where there is no livestock to graze this grassland, it can grow very tall and accumulate the dry chaff from many years running.

A fire in grasslands moves so rapidly it can be difficult for firefighters to keep up with the flames. Fast-moving fires tend to burn at lower temperatures and the soil cools more quickly after the flames pass. Firescaping in grasslands is much easier than other plant communities because the uncultivated areas may be either grazed, mowed, or cultivated, all of which practically eliminate fuel availability. However, grass completely renews itself each year, which means management of this fuel must be done faithfully after each spring growth spurt.

On flat ground, grassland fire has less potential to dry the ornamental plants in green belts because flames in grass tend to be shorter in stature and burn for a limited time. Grass fires in hill country are more dangerous to residences in canyons where temperatures rise quickly, or those perched on the edges of ridge tops receiving the brunt of rising heat and embers. Due to the diversity of terrain coupled with the tendency for spotted brushy growth, grassland fires can be fast moving and sometimes unpredictable.

SAGEBRUSH-GRASS

Throughout much of the inland west, many variations of sagebrush plant communities develop in areas of poor soil, on lower mountain slopes, or where grassland has been degraded allowing brush to intermix with sparse grass. Original pure sagebrush areas were limited by fire because the shrubs could not tolerate the annual burning so beneficial to grass. As the West was settled, prairie fires were suppressed, and livestock grazing became widespread. This combined to weaken the pure stands of grasses enough for the sagebrush to gain a foothold and begin a gradual invasion. This is a prime example of how a transition between two recognized vegetation types has created a new classification all its own. Over the last century grasslands throughout the West have been degraded by sage into the new class called sagebrush-grass.

Fires in sagebrush-grass areas burn as fast as grass fires, over six miles per hour in some cases. They also burn far hotter due to the woody stems, twigs, and sage oils, making them difficult to control. These fires also produce sizeable embers that can be wind borne to start spot fires beyond the main fire line. Homesites in many rural western subdivisions

This example shows some of the smaller species of sagebrush found throughout the West. The amount of grass present will vary according to climate and soils. Sagebrush is not fire resistant and cannot resprout once burned. This is why sagebrush was limited to areas outside the grasslands, which burned almost every year. Today with the suppression of fire, it is not uncommon to find a greater abundance of sagebrush invading grasslands than ever before.

Fire is an important element in ponderosa pine forests and this example shows what happened after a fire burned off the dense vegetation. The following spring the hillside bloomed in *Lillium humboldtii*, a native tiger lily that is all but vanished from the west slope. This proves lack of fire is leading to their extinction due to unchecked brush cover and shade.

surrounded with sagebrush-grass plant communities are at greater risk than those on grassland alone. In addition, there is less opportunity to use livestock to graze away the fire danger as they do not browse on the pungent sage.

PONDEROSA PINE FOREST

The majestic ponderosa pine blankets millions of acres from the Dakotas to Arizona, California's Sierra Nevada to Colorado. Ponderosa pine stands encountered by the early explorers were described as open and parklike. This was due to the frequent ground fires that were started by lightning or Native Americans, who burned for a variety of reasons. Large landscape fires burned irregularly in a patchwork pattern called "mosaic" every two to twenty-five years. This fire decreased the number of plants competing with ponderosas for the limited water and nutrients in their arid natural habitat.

Much of today's ponderosa pine wildland has lost its open appearance and is now choked with shrubs, seedlings, and saplings to make parts of the forest impenetrable. This is primarily a result of fire suppression, which allowed most of the new seedlings to sprout and mature. This overcrowding was also due to some nineteenth-century logging that allowed less drought-tolerant firs to replace what was once pure ponderosa pine stands. The firs are susceptible to drought and become stressed allowing various pests and diseases to invade the trees. Similar cases are occurring throughout the West with altered forests struggling to survive and losing the battle. Badly damaged by pests, what remains of the forest is highly vulnerable to fire.

Crowded ponderosa pine stands, or mixtures of pine and fir today represent some of our most volatile forest ecosystems, and in recent years fires there have defied control. One 600-year-old ponderosa pine in the Boise National Forest managed to escape fire for six centuries, but burned to death in the 1992 Foothills Fire. This illustrates how our altered forests overwhelm natural fire resistance in ponderosa pine and other mature trees. No longer are the fires similar to those set by the Indians, they are today deadly, fast moving, incredibly hot, and unpredictable.

MIXED FIR

Mixed firs which include Douglas fir, grand fir, cedar, and other conifers are typically found in higher elevations of mountain ranges of the West or along the Pacific Coast where summer temperatures are cooler. Fires in these ecosystems burned anywhere from twenty- to as much as 150-year intervals. With such a long time span between burns, these forests can become naturally crowded and fires range from light ground fires to huge stand-replacing wildfires.

Despite this fire history, homes here are not as vulnerable to wildfire. This is in part because development tends to cluster in low foothill areas where topography is more gentle. However, when drought and extreme weather do generate a fire, homes nestled in deep forest, canyons, and inaccessible sites are almost indefensible.

This forest is typical of those where firs have invaded areas outside their normal range due to the absence of fire. Many people are moving in to these picturesque ecosystems and have no idea of the fuel accumulations.

LODGEPOLE PINE

Lodgepole pine is a fire-dependent tree and gets its name from the long gently tapering trunks used as supports for Native American tepees. Lodgepole develops dense stands of columnar trees all of similar age. When the stand grows old and decadent at about fifty to eighty years of age, they become vulnerable to lightning fires. If no lightning fires occur, the native mountain pine beetle kills most of the trees, but these remain standing or down and dead indefinitely. Eventually these dead stands will burn in intense, high temperature wildfires. After the fire, old cones open and distribute seed on the wind which quickly takes root in the thick bed of nutritious ash left by the fire. Lodgepole seedlings are the fastest growers of all the pine clan.

Like the mixed fir forests, lodgepole pine is common in and around Rocky Mountain communities and those of other ranges in western states. Homes are naturally vulnerable because the stand will age and die, and houses in and around them will be threatened when the stand burns. It is essential that anyone living in lodgepole pine country be highly aware of the number of trees around the house, their density, health, and age.

DIFFICULT DECISIONS

The ideal solution to the forest health problem caused by exclusion of fire is to implement programs of selective logging and prescribed burning. Unfortunately foresters are prevented from carrying out both of these measures by environmental restrictions, habitat preservation, and other public concerns. In addition just how and when to burn has always presented a dilemma.

The general belief among some is to simply leave the forests untouched because nature will take care of the problem. But nature has already been altered in most cases, even though we perceive these forests as pristine. In theory, hands-off preservation may seem like a wise decision, but in fact it has actually contributed to forest decline. If involved in a wildfire today, the forests will burn so intensely that even the fire-resistant species will have no chance of survival.

Homes located within these forests are vulnerable to crown fires, which travel through the tops of trees and move very quickly. When it

MISCELLANEOUS BRUSHLAND ECOSYSTEMS

Logging and lack of fire has for the past one hundred fifty years changed the face of many ecosystems in Western states. It has allowed shrubs and brush to invade once open forests creating a two-layer supply of fuels. The upper layer is tree canopies, the lower layer is shrubs mixed with tree seedlings, a layer both woody and very dense. When the ground fuels and the canopies burn together, the combined fire is so hot it becomes difficult to extinguish, particularly were steep terrain makes access difficult.

In California and parts of Arizona a native brushland called "chaparral" fuels intense fires at elevations from about 1,000 feet up to 4,000 feet, although this varies depending on location relative to mountain ranges and exposures. Chaparral is a fire-dependent ecosystem, but since fire suppression it has become overgrown, decadent, and extremely volatile because these native shrubs contain a higher than normal amount of flammable oils.

In eastern Oregon, Washington, and New Mexico brushland includes dwarf conifer woodlands that are comprised of drought-tolerant piñon, juniper, and limber pine. Grazing, logging, and, most importantly, lack of fire have caused these and other similar brushy ecosystems to become far more dense than they grew under the natural fire regimes. What was once a low-fire area has become highly volatile, and because of the pitch in these species they tend to burn much the same way as chaparral.

Brushland fires are some of our most devastating for the following reasons:

1. Topography is usually steep and rolling.

2. Canopy and ground fuel loads are extremely high due to density of vegetation.

3. Fire burns longer and hotter than grass fires.

4. Roadways (or lack of them) often limit access.

5. Houses tend to be built for views that make them difficult to defend due to hillside and ridgetop locations.

Dense second growth thickets of scrub oak, manzanita, and other native shrubs of the Sierra Nevada illustrate the problems with accessibility when homes are in or around steep wall canyons.

In a fast-moving fire, brush may not be totally consumed as these manzanita skeletons prove. But in recent years, burns have been so hot they move very quickly and leave nothing but ash in their wake.

drops to the ground, the fire feeds upon the accumulations of litter, dead twigs, branches, and leaves. If there is sufficient litter, the organic matter within the soil may burn and the elusive ground fire will begin to smolder, sterilizing the earth by consuming nutrient-rich duff.

The sight of a fifty-foot pine tree fully engulfed in flame is a humbling experience. Imagine the survival prospects of a home only twenty feet tall surrounded by dozens of flaming pines; the radiant heat so great the air is no longer breathable. If the pine needle litter is also burning, the flames move quickly to the structure, consuming all combustible material in its path.

Many of these forests are in steep terrain, far from civilization, with the only hope of containment being aerial bombardment. But even then, firefighters know it is often mother nature who ultimately decides where and when the fire is stopped. Increased frequency and intensity of fires, isolated home sites, narrow winding roads, and low populations reduce the ability to fight forest fires. This illustrates how essential it is for residents to create their own defensible space if there is to be any chance of saving the home.

URBAN FORESTS

As California's Oakland Firestorm proved in 1991, there are other sorts of wildfires that are not related to native ecosystems. During this devastating fire, homes clustered in well-populated areas burned because the structures and the surrounding landscaping provided sufficient fuel to create a crown fire condition. The wind and other factors contributed to a firestorm that raged through the homes at an incredible rate. There was little hope of putting out such a fire, driven by relentless dry winds into tinder-dry, drought-stricken landscapes. This control problem was compounded by the fact that the Oakland Hills are accessed by a series of narrow, winding streets that traversed some very steep slopes.

Researcher Tim Payson of the Riverside Forest Fire Lab feels strongly that the urban forest fire presents nearly as great a hazard as fires in wildlands. Imagine an urban neighborhood of single-family dwellings closely spaced and surrounded by dehydrated landscape trees. In older communities the roofing material may be wood shingles or shakes, which ignite easily and develop crown fire conditions. Add stepping stones of drought-desiccated landscape trees between houses and you have the worst fuel-loading conditions of a forest or chaparral fire.

This urban forest fire is not restricted to wood-roofed houses. One firefighter watched sparks lodge in the open ends of tile roofs to begin burning the homes around the eaves. In older neighborhoods where vegetation has matured, as in Oakland, droughts and hot summer winds create a deadly situation wherever you live. This shows that increased consciousness of our very real fire threat must be realized by both rural and urban dwellers alike.

2

YOUR HOME AND HOMESITE: SELECTION, STRUCTURES, AND INSURANCE

The western United States is facing a serious problem that has been building for nearly a century. Forests and wildland vegetation are stressed and over-crowded, making them highly vulnerable to fire from natural and manmade causes from increased residential development in outlying areas. Foresters have been predicting the advent of these big burns for some time now, but it was not until the disastrous fall of 2017 that their warnings became a horrible reality.

Accepting the fact that homes in the urban-wildland interface will be threatened by fire at one time or another, those with greatest chances of survival must be properly located, constructed of resistant materials, and the site suitable for creating defensible space. Defensible space is a managed area around a home with limited fuel availability, which helps to reduce the intensity and speed of a fire. It also provides a place for firefighters to take a stand when protecting your house. Homes or homesites that cannot meet this criteria are not a good investment in and around fire-prone ecosystems.

Regardless of how much homeowner's fire insurance you carry, there is no amount of money that will make up for the losses of a lifetime—the baby pictures, the clock your grandfather made, the family heirloom silver. Those who dismiss the threat of fire because of sizeable insurance policies are playing a dangerous game. For there is always the more serious threat that someone may be injured or killed, a loss that no insurance policy can compensate.

HUNTING DOWN A DEFENSIBLE HOMESITE

The best way to protect yourself against a vulnerable homesite is to avoid purchasing one. A vast number of new and resale homes in rural parts of the western and southeastern United States are at great risk of fire. The more rural the site, the greater potential of wildfire. But if you know what to look for in a bare lot or home, you will be able to sort through the properties to find the most defensible one.

New subdivisions are typically created from a larger tract of land. The lots of the subdivision may range in size from a city lot to small ranches of numerous acres. In many fire-conscious areas, cities and county planning departments are requiring these subdivisions provide adequate access for firefighting equipment and demand there be water hydrants at various points within the development. Some areas even require each homesite to store a designated amount of water and a delivery system that ties into interior ceiling sprinklers.

Most rural residential planning agencies do not have these requirements with their subdivision planning process, and in this case each homesite relies on its own domestic well for water. Some of these wells produce as little as two gallons per minute, hardly sufficient for even daily household needs much less fire protection. Without a community water source, there is rarely a dose, accessible water supply for firefighting efforts in dry parts. When house or property hunting, always keep this water availability issue in mind.

Firefighting agencies vary according to where you live. In the most rural areas, such as the Cascades, the Wasach and Rocky Mountains, and other small ranges, there is only the US Forest Service and state firefighting agency stations widely distributed in remote areas. These organizations are designed to control wildland fires and keep them away from residential areas or single isolated homes. Some fire agencies arrive on the scene of a structure fire in order to prevent the flames from igniting surrounding vegetation.

It's also important to understand what protecting a home means to firefighters whose major goal is to stop the advance of a wildfire. They have a limited number of men in each crew to work the fire line, and each time a home comes in reach of the fire, a few men must pull off the fire

FIRESCAPING TIP

With the efforts of firefighters so desperately needed on the fire line, it's essential for you the homeowner to have some means of fighting your own fires. By the time a volunteer fire department reaches your home, chances are it will already be engulfed in flames. A fire-safe homesite and building is the best way to prevent a house fire or ignition from a wildfire. To fight either structure or wildland fires yourself, a private water supply and the proper firefighting equipment is the best investment you will ever make.

line to protect the home. That leaves fewer firefighters to actually fight the fire. If homes are defensible and well equipped with firefighting systems, there is less demand on the fire crew manpower.

In rural areas the role of fighting structure fires falls to the county firefighting agencies, and in most cases it is the local volunteer fire department. This is made up of citizens who volunteer their efforts to fight fires because local government agencies cannot provide a fulltime station close enough to their communities. But despite the efforts of these dedicated volunteers, they must be notified of the fire, drive to the fire station, and then reach the home or property with their equipment. It's easy to see this is not the most expedient firefighting arrangement, but it is better than the alternative—none at all. In some states each volunteer fire department is rated according to the speed of their response on a scale of 1 to 10, with 10 being the fastest. This rating is used to figure the cost of home fire insurance policies in that area.

When looking for a home in a new area, inquire at the nearest fire station about its capability, and whether it is permanently staffed or volunteer. Note how far the station is from your home and the conditions of the roadways in route. Don't forget that fires sometimes occur in the winter too, when snow or mud may complicate access. Find out where the nearest state forestry station is from the homesite as well.

QUALITIES OF A DEFENSIBLE HOMESITE

1. Topography

Avoid homes or lots on hillsides or steep cut-and-fill sloping subdivisions. Fire tends to burn more quickly on hillsides, and these sites are more difficult for firefighters to surround and protect from oncoming flames. Deep canyons, particularly if choked with vegetation are equally as risky, with even greater difficulty for access than on slopes. You should be able to clear and manage an area least one hundred feet on all sides of your home and not be dependent on your neighbor's attention to clearing for the safety of your homesite. Some homesites are so difficult to defend that insurance companies may become reluctant or even refuse to write a policy for them.

2. Wildland Interface

Avoid homes adjacent to open space that cannot be managed to reduce fire danger. For example, the residents of Laguna Beach, California were subjected to greater hazards due to the restrictions by wildlife agencies

Although it is a view lot, this home is still standing because it was set back from the edge of the slope with plenty of access on all sides for firefighters and their equipment. It is constructed of stucco with a tile roof, and probably has double-pane windows. There are also no trees close to the building, and virtually none on the sloping sides either.

on grazing or prescribed burning of open space "habitat." One way to find out is to obtain the Environmental Impact Report for the subdivision through the local planning department and read the biology reports it contains. If there are references to endangered species of any kind, beware, as this is the chief legislation which hampers vegetation management of any kind and binds the hands of firefighting agencies. But where older subdivisions are concerned, the EIR may not exist or be outdated. You may contact your state's Department of Fish and Game or the US Fish and Wildlife Service for their reports on the surrounding area and whether it is currently considered habitat for an endangered species or likely to become so in the future.

3. Access

Many rural communities have a network of poorly signed roads, some paved, others just gravel. The unpaved roads can be county maintained, but some subdivisions share communal private roads maintained by the residents it serves as a group. Homeowners' associations of this sort can be rife with disagreement, particularly when they discover how expensive it is to keep a road in good shape. Road maintenance requires regular grading with heavy equipment, addition of road-base gravel and reconstruction of drainage features that prevent wash-outs and pot holes.

When culverts and bridges are involved, it can really get sticky. A bridge capable of supporting firefighting trucks must be built to withstand at least forty thousand pounds of weight (twenty tons). If one or more of the group refuse to contribute their share to the road maintenance work, the others may be forced to make up the difference.

Access also relates to the width of the road or your own driveway. Some rural driveways can be unusually long or steep as they are not governed by roadway construction limits established by state transportation departments, the county, or city. Sharp curves may be impossible for fire trucks to maneuver. Over time, natural vegetation may narrow the shoulders of the road and although your car may have no difficulty managing it, the firefighting trucks could be prevented from entering. Also, imagine a driveway with encroaching vegetation totally aflame on both sides. This picture does not make evacuation or access by firefighters seem possible.

Think long and hard about the work required to clear brush for 10 feet on either side of your private road or five feet for a driveway every year that you own the home.

Yet another issue which frequently confronts firefighters is the single-lane driveway. If an evacuating family is exiting through this conduit, the firefighters heading toward the flames will meet the other vehicle head on, and will have to back down the road until it is wide enough to pass, then go forward again. This delay might be just long enough to prevent them from saving your house.

Rural residents often joke about the convoluted directions to find a house in isolated back-country communities. "Turn left at the third tree after the red reflector just 1.3 miles off the main road," is an example of

ENCROACHING VEGETATION   ROADWAY WIDE ENOUGH FOR TWO-WAY TRAFFIC   10′ CLEAR ZONE

Road or Driveway Cross Section

A typical road lane is 12 feet across, a two-way road at least 24 feet across. In snow country this may be even wider to allow a grader through. There must be room to pass an oncoming car or fire truck by using that extra space. Treatment of the vegetation adjacent to the road is essential if it is to remain open when a fire sweeps through. If the vegetation shown on the left side was to be similar on the opposite side of the road, it could become a tunnel of fire. The 10-foot clear zone shown on the right is a minimum, and if an even greater area can be cleared, the access will be safer.

what it takes to find some of these places. Firefighters have an equally hard time finding your house under these conditions without clear road signs and address numbers. Most people make the mistake of never learning their street address when there is no rural mail delivery. The number of your house and that of your neighbors' helps police and firefighters to find your home in case of emergency. Be sure it is prominently displayed.

4. Emergency Water

Water is a scarce commodity in many parts of the West, but it is essential if you are to be able to fight fires at your rural home. Of course, in communities with built-in fire water systems need not be as concerned about this factor, unless the hydrant is a long distance from your homesite. There is plenty more in chapter 4 on this subject, but for now it is sufficient to know that a homesite that has its own water supply and storage system is a thousand times more valuable than one that does not.

Natural sources include springs and streams, but be sure to evaluate their output or levels during the late summer and fall when some may dry up completely. Remember this is the time of year that water is the most needed. Ponds or swimming pools are other good water reservoirs, but pond water levels may fluctuate depending on whether they are fed by streams, springs, or seasonal irrigation ditch water. Domestic wells are rated by their gallons per minute, and low output cannot be relied upon because some will become exhausted during prolonged droughts, or if pumped constantly over long periods. Limited supply can be compensated for by swimming pools or large water tanks, but both are expensive to buy and install. Think long and hard about this feature of your new or existing site, because a dry home is likely to become a burned home.

BUILDINGS AND MATERIALS

A house may be able to better resist nearby wildland fires if it is constructed properly. This relates primarily to roofing, but there are other factors such as design which also contribute to this ability to deter ignition. The major offender in every case is the wood shake or shingle roof, and sometimes siding of the same material. Older neighborhoods may have many homes with this kind of roofing; most newer rural communities strictly forbid them. If your home has shingles on the siding or roof, consider it highly vulnerable to fire, and even though the material may have been treated to make it less flammable, this chemical will gradually disappear after just a few years.

Roof material has a lot do with a defensible home. Most fire insurance companies require roofing Class C or better before they write a policy. New legislation and building codes are likely to demand only Class A in high hazard areas. Roofing materials are rated as follows:

Class A Maximum Protection

Clay tiles, concrete tiles, fiberglass shingles, metal tiles, perlite shakes, Class-A-rated pressure-treated cedar shakes, built-up roof (9 layers fiberglass).

Class B Moderate Protection

Class-B-rated pressure-treated cedar shakes, metal tiles, built-up roof (7 layers).

Class C Minimum Protection

Asphalt shingles, built-up roof (3 layers), Class-C pressure-treated cedar shakes.

Non-Rated

Avoid any roofing materials with less than a Class C rating and those that have no rating.

FIRESCAPING TIP

Although your home may be roofed with a Class-A-rated material, its effectiveness may be influenced by how well sealed the edges are. Sparks and embers tend to lodge in nooks and crannies of roofing. Tile roofs often have openings just above the fascia or rain gutters. Roofs of this type have been known to ignite and burn beneath the tiles from embers that entered through these openings. Fire experts insist these be closed off with suitable filler material for maximum Class A benefit.

SPRAY-ON TREATMENTS—WHAT FIRE CHIEFS SAY

There is some confusion as to the effectiveness of spray-on treatments for wood roofing. Unscrupulous contractors may not always be truthful about every aspect of their products. Consider the following facts gathered by experienced fire chiefs:

1. No spray-on application has passed standard tests recognized by the fire and building code agencies. Demand copies of test results from Underwriter's Laboratories or building code agencies if indicated by seller. Double check these at your nearest fire station.
2. Flame-spread ratings and treatments are applicable only to materials used in the interior of buildings.
3. Guarantees usually do not assure fire resistance but refer to a respray if material fails (a lot of good that is with no house left).
4. Cleaning the roof prior to application may cause cracking of shakes and shingles from foot traffic or water pressure from equipment. Replacement of wood roofs with Class A materials is the only realistic means of reducing the hazard.

The siding of your house is another potentially combustible material. Views of some burned communities show large sheets of stucco siding still intact, while the roofs and wood studs that surrounded them were burned to ashes. Stucco and masonry are always better than wood siding. The thicker these materials are applied, the less heat they absorb and the greater the insulation factor.

Vents that allow air exchange in attics and crawl spaces also make the house vulnerable. Sparks enter attics through these openings, or through foundation ventilation openings, to ignite the beams and materials beneath your floors. The more vents, as well as other nooks and crannies in the architecture, the greater opportunity there is for an ember to lodge and ignite the materials around it. It is recommended that all vents be covered with a non-flammable ¼-inch mesh screen.

The fire ignited the roof of this house and the flames spread throughout the interior, consuming all the wood structure. All that is left is the exterior wall stucco, which crumbled with its support burned.

Windows can also transmit heat from outdoor flames into the house, particularly if they are facing hillsides or masses of vegetation that burn unusually hot. The larger the window the greater the danger. Drapes and furnishings inside the house can actually catch fire through single-pane windows. Double-pane windows are recommended for a more fire-resistant home. They have greater insulating qualities and are less subject to breaking when exposed to high temperatures.

Another vulnerable part of the house is the eaves. Open eaves that leave the ends of roof joists exposed are thin and become hot very quickly. Embers rising from burning vegetation around the house tend to gather underneath them. All eaves should be no deeper than absolutely necessary, which may conflict with some of the solar-heat calculations required by building departments for greater energy efficiency. To comply with building codes, box in the eaves. Regardless of the scale of existing or proposed eaves, they should always be tightly boxed in with fire-resistant materials.

INSURANCE

In the past, some homeowners purposefully undervalued their homes when buying fire insurance to lower the premiums. Although they may have saved a few dollars each month, many people found this was penny wise and pound foolish after their house burned to the ground. Afterwards they discovered there was no hope of building a new house with the limited amount paid by the insurance company.

If these homeowners had approached the problem of cost in more logical terms, they might have discovered that increasing the deductible may have saved just as much money. For example, an annual premium with $100 deductible may cost roughly double that of the same coverage with a $2,500 deductible. It is the total devastation of a home that few can recover from on their own; the first few thousand dollars of damage can be resolved by personal loans or payment plans. Therefore, it is far wiser to reduce insurance premiums by raising the deductible rather than undervaluing the house.

The problem of being underinsured is usually overlooked by the homeowner for other reasons. Perhaps the most common is that real estate in many western states, such as Washington, Oregon and Colorado, has skyrocketed in value due to the Internet during the last two decades. This is true of prime lots in affluent suburbs within commuting distance from cities such as Spokane, Boise, or Boulder. It's also a problem in mountain resort communities such as Park City and Aspen. A second factor is that new home construction is subjected to far more costly regulations today than in the past. For example, indoor fire sprinklers, insulation, roofing, window type and quantity, heating and air conditioning are all more expensive to install, not due to inflation, but because of building department standards. The heavy regulation of the logging industry has also driven the cost of lumber into the stratosphere, so rebuilding with wood is now more costly than ever.

In the event your home does burn, it's essential you carry sufficient fire insurance with a policy that covers a number of important factors. If you already have a policy, review it and make appropriate adjustments in order to be sure you are adequately covered. And every year that the policy is renewed, review it again just to be sure you are not left underinsured in the event of disaster.

IMPORTANT FACTORS TO CONSIDER WHEN BUYING FIRE INSURANCE

1. Replacement Costs

If you purchased your home twenty years ago for $100,000, chances are your insurance policy was written to provide a replacement value of that amount. But if you were lucky, today the same home may be worth $250,000. It's easy to see that a policy must be updated as property values rise in order to provide an accurate replacement value. Everyone should look at his or her policy and determine what that amount actually is. If it is lower than the home's current value, which can be estimated by your insurance agent, then you should increase your policy limits. Be sure to make adjustments for improvements such as installation of a swimming pool, redwood deck, or remodeling.

2. Building Standards

Today's city and county building departments are growing more strict about construction methods and materials allowed in home building. Energy regulations restrict the number, size, and type of windows. They may also dictate the efficiency rating of air conditioning and heating units as well as insulation. Where there was once no criteria regarding roofing material, there may now be only Class A allowed in your neighborhood. Class A can be more expensive in two ways: the materials cost more and special structural provisions are required in the roof framing system to accommodate additional weight. More subtle changes in the Uniform Building Code add nickel-and-dime costs to the price of a new house. Put them all together and you discover replacement cost applies not only to inflation, but to the rising price of conforming to new regulations and codes.

3. Personal Possessions

Insurance policies cover not only the building, but its contents as well. Police departments recommend homeowners document their possessions in the event of burglary, but this is also a good idea in case of fire. Furniture, audiovisual equipment, computers, and anything else of value is worth documenting with a home video camera or by still photos. Take the information to your insurance agent and discuss whether the "personal contents" section of your policy adequately covers these items. Special policies are available for fine art, jewelry, furs, or rare antiques. For smaller items a fire-resistant box or safe may keep them more accessible than a bank safe deposit box, and for less money than an insurance policy.

Homeowner's policies don't always cover home offices, which may contain costly high-tech equipment, records, and files which may be impossible to replace. The losses may completely destroy the business. For adequate coverage take out a small business owner's policy that includes liability coverage.

4. Living Expenses

We all have a tendency to file away our policies without ever having read all the details. One aspect of a home fire policy is its provisions for your living expenses until you find a new home. This is a finite amount, and if you plan to rebuild it may be a year or longer before you can move into the new house. Find out exactly what your policy provides for living expenses, and if you think more coverage would be needed, discuss this with your agent. Remember, if your house burns to the ground, as most do in wildfire scenarios, you will be left with little or nothing. Getting back on your feet may be overwhelmingly expensive.

5. Site Improvements

Insurance policies covering city homes are fairly straightforward, but when it comes to rural properties there are other things to be considered. Wildfires burn more than just homes; they destroy fencing, irrigation systems, outbuildings, garden or farm equipment, and unfortunately livestock too. There is a difference in price, as well as coverage, between farm or ranch insurance policies and those strictly for homes.

If your home is rural but not a working farm or ranch, it is wise to discuss any site improvements with your agent to find out if they are covered. For example, if you have recreational horses and a stable that may contain expensive tack and equipment, it would be difficult to replace these yourself if burned by a wildfire and not covered by your insurance policy. It's a good idea to buy an additional endorsement for these items as well as the horses if they are expensive show-quality animals. This also

UNDERSTANDING INSURANCE TERMS

Guaranteed replacement cost Replacement cost is based on a fixed amount dictated by the policy, and provides no additional funds under any circumstances. Guaranteed replacement is more open-ended and will cover your property even if it exceeds the policy limit. Understandably, this type of coverage costs you higher premiums.

Inflation-guard clause This clause assures you the policy is readjusted each year upon renewal to cover increases in local construction costs. It factors in both changes in building standards and inflation rates.

Actual cash value This figure is calculated by insurance companies by factoring in depreciation in finding the value of your house.

Endorsement If there is additional coverage over and above the basic policy, an endorsement of the terms will be attached to the main policy. This is where you will find specialized coverage of high tech equipment, art, antiques or jewelry, as well as many other unusual items of value.

applies to fencing, especially if decorative, because replacement may be very expensive, particularly on a large scale. Other rural improvements which should be covered in your policy include: domestic well house and equipment, sheds, barns, outdoor electrical lines/lighting, and irrigation systems.

Farm and ranch policies are designed to cover these things as well as the farmer's commodities, such as orchards, stored feed, haystacks, general livestock, tack, farming equipment, large barns, and harvested crops. Special endorsements may apply to purebred livestock such as a breeding bull or stallion, which may be valued at tens of thousands of dollars. The insurance agent will require a value assessment of items to be covered, then write the policy based on this information.

HOW INSURANCE COMPANIES RATE FIRE DANGER

Insurance companies use a safety rating system to establish the fire insurance premium of homes in suburban or rural areas. It takes into consideration surrounding vegetation, topography, housing density, fire history, water availability, and local ordinances, all factors relating to the vulnerability of a home or homesite. Insurance companies in fire-prone areas are likely to adopt this system or a similar one very soon. Consider these issues when evaluating an existing home or preparing to buy a new one.

In this system, the lower the total score, the safer the homesite. A score of 7 to 10 is considered high-risk. Where does your neighborhood fit in?

Danger Points

Grass, weeds; shrubs + 1
Large shrubs, small trees +2
Timber woodlands +3
1- to 10-degree slope + 1
10- to 20-degree slope + 2
20- to 40-degree slope + 3
40-degree slope or more +4
Less than 1 home per 10 acres + 1
1 home per 5 to 10 acres +2
1 home per 0 to 5 acres +3
Rough terrain + 1
History of fire + 1
Extreme fire weather + 1

Safety Points

Good water, roads, signs -1
Strict local fire ordinances -1

3

THE UNIQUE TRIANGLE: WIND, TEMPERATURE, HUMIDITY

Toward the end of summer, the hills turn brown and the wildland trees and shrubs settle into their best drought-survival mode until relieved by the fickle rains of fall. If water supplies are low, plants in landscapes of homes are equally dry, leaves desiccated, moisture content low, and many that could not stand the water denial have died. During these dog days the heat hangs low upon the land, air so dry it feels like a sprinkling of talcum powder upon the skin. Evenings are balmy and warm, lakes and rivers beckon, and the activity of early summer has exhausted itself into a quiet peace.

Lurking beneath this bucolic scene is the ever-present threat of fires, and many rural residents refuse to utter the word in superstitious fear, while others knock on wood. Fire weather relies on three conditions: wind, high temperatures, and low humidity. Whether or not there is a fire also depends on the availability of fuel.

It is easy to see why most people grow nervous when fire season begins. The forests and national parks are filled with camping tourists, many naively careless and unfamiliar with wildland fire etiquette. Arsonists tend to grow more excited under these conditions knowing their efforts have the greatest chance of becoming a serious wildfire. Everyone should stay tuned to their local news and frequently scan the skies for the plumes of smoke that mark the start of a "big one." This is when it is most important for everyone to be extra cautious about any activity that could possibly ignite a fire.

WIND

The prevailing summer winds in most western states are not serious fire-driving winds, although they can be hot and dry. But in late summer and early autumn, the sun often heats the surface of the soil and the air above it so completely that a pressure difference occurs. As air moves from higher pressure zones to those of lower pressure, wind results. The direction of these winds varies, and to get a good picture of your local wind patterns consult the experts at a nearby fire station.

In mountain and foothill areas—anything from gentle rolling hills to heavily vegetated, nearly vertical cliffs—winds eddy in undulating topography. With each day of wind, plants and surrounding grasslands grow drier as moisture is literally drawn out of the leaves. Fires driven by these winds can move so rapidly over such a large area they easily become uncontrollable. In recent scenarios of the inland West fires burn until the winds die down or the onset of rain and snowfall.

Other versions of these same winds can blow over higher elevations in our mountain ranges during late summer. This is made even more dangerous because they are associated with afternoon thunderheads that produce violent lightning storms. Sometimes rain follows, but often it does not, and lighting has historically been the natural fire starter in our native forest ecosystems.

Wind also has a big impact on the fire danger closer to coastal communities. The vegetation just a few miles from the beach can be very dense due to high rainfall and the perpetual moisture-laden breezes coming off the ocean. But when an inversion occurs the wind blows in the opposite direction. Wind originates on the hot, sunbaked inland plains and blows out to sea, and in the process it rapidly dries out coastal forest lands. Because these forests are not usually considered fire danger areas, homesites are unprotected. Though rare, coastal fires can be very difficult to control due to limited access, low population, and widely scattered homesites as evidenced in the 140,000-acre Ojai to Santa Barbara in December 2017.

TEMPERATURE

In almost every major fire, the weather was hot and daily temperatures consistently high. Heat from a flame will travel much further in warmer conditions than in cooler temperatures. For example, a neighbor had safely burned a pile of old board fencing in his field during the winter months. He accumulated a second, nearly identical pile of the same material by the middle of summer. But when he burned it on a warm afternoon the heat became far more intense, radiating out over a much bigger circle around the burn pile. In fact, it became so hot the paint on his home blistered and he feared it would ignite before the burn pile could be extinguished. The single difference in these two fires was ambient air temperature.

Another factor relating to temperature is the state of plants, both native and introduced species. Evapotranspiration is a word used to describe the combined evaporation of moisture from both the soil surface and the leaves of a plant. In high temperatures, especially over weeks or months at a time, the evapotranspiration rate increases and plants lose vital moisture. As soil moisture evaporates to deeper and deeper levels, the reservoir available to plants diminishes.

Plants that have evolved with a resistance to drought conditions have deep root systems which access soil moisture during these high-stress periods. But under prolonged heat they too will eventually consume all soil moisture and then turn to other methods of survival such as dormancy or defoliation. Plants less adapted to drought will die.

Plants subjected to heat and lack of moisture first cease to grow because there is insufficient water to carry on photosynthesis. Desert cacti evolved a unique mechanism of lying dormant during the day, their

FIRESCAPING TIP

Fire experts tell us a campfire in 40-degree air warms an area about two feet on all sides. That same fire in 90-degree summer temperatures warms an area twenty feet on all sides. Evaluate the size and influence of your burn pile accordingly.

surface pores tightly dosed against moisture loss in the heat. After sunset their pores, or stomata, open in order to begin photosynthesis during the night using stored light energy. But most plants are not so rugged.

The next drought mechanism causes plants to wilt because they do not contain sufficient moisture to keep the turgidity, or water pressure, up to par within their vessels. After that, the plant will defoliate by dropping all its leaves to reduce the foliage demand for moisture. Without leaves some plants die, but others become temporarily dormant such as Western natives do until fall rains support a new crop of leaves. When plants die or defoliate they add that much more dry, volatile fuel for fires.

HUMIDITY

Humidity is a term that refers to the amount of suspended moisture in the air. Coastal communities are perpetually moist, not because of rainfall, but due to the proximity of a large body of water. Air moisture is supplied by surface evaporation of water vapor from the soil, water bodies and through transpiration of plants. **Relative humidity** is gauged by determining how much moisture the air could hold if it were saturated. Rain is close to 100 percent saturation, but, in contrast, many recent fire-weather scenarios registered less than 20 percent humidity. The daily humidity percentages are usually mentioned on radio or television weather broadcasts.

Water vapor remains in the air longer at lower temperatures. As heat increases it tends to dry up and humidity levels drop. This was evident in the 2018 Mendocino Complex Fire that grew out of the Cage fire to become the largest fire in California history at over 400,000 acres that continued to burn until rainfall finally put it out. While this and many other fires covered the whole state in late July, the humidity was high and winds minimal in the southland, and yet the whole state blew up in wildfire far earlier than ever before. Thus we know now that large damaging fires are occurring earlier and more frequently than ever.

This is how temperature and humidity are interrelated. Dead fuels, such as leaf litter, dry grass, twigs, and pine cones, usually contain a significant amount of moisture in humid conditions, but when humidity decreases this stuff slowly dries out to become a volatile fuel. This is the case in coastal forests of the Pacific Northwest, which can be devastated by the humidity drop caused by inland winds punching through to the coast.

HOW MOST WILDFIRES ARE STARTED

It is sad to say, but many of our worst fires were set intentionally by arsonists. These "torches" tend to become more active during fire weather or when other wildfires are already burning. In many cases the arsonist is fascinated by fire and remains on the scene to observe the flames. Sometimes he or she will actually help firefighters. Police understand these and many other characteristics of arsonists and keep a sharp eye out on every fire scene for suspicious individuals.

Other fires are caused by negligence. This refers to people who know they are not supposed to burn rubbish, but do so anyway. Another example is "sneaking" a campfire after dark, when the smoke isn't visible, even when the forest rangers have made it clear fires are prohibited. Sometimes smokers will be careless in high-fire-hazard wildlands, or toss a burning ember out the car window. All these fires can be avoided if people are cautious of fire danger and act accordingly.

FIRESCAPING TIP

It is ironic that many grass fires ore started by conscientious homeowners trying to mow down dry grass around their homes in the late summer to reduce fire hazard. This becomes a "damned if you do—damned if you don't" situation. If you do mow there's a chance of equipment starting a fire; but if you don't mow, there's enough fuel present to burn down your home. Fire experts say the time to mow is much earlier in the year, while grass is still green and less combustible. Fires ignite when tinder-dry clippings make contact with a hot engine or exhaust system. Sparks ore also produced when the blade of a rotary mower or a flail mower hits rocks or dirt, a factor more insidious because it occurs out of sight beneath the mower blade housing.

THE TEN MOST COMMON SOURCES OF WILDFIRES

The following represent the most frequent known causes of wildfire ignition. Be doubly cautious of these during fire season.

I. Equipment use
   Examples: heavy equipment, farm implements, power tools.

2. Vehicles
   Examples: recreational vehicles, automobiles, trucks, 4x4s. Beware when pulling off the road onto a shoulder where dry grass and weeds come in contact with your automobile. Avoid off-road vehicle activity during fire season, particularly hunting during dry years.

3. Arson

4. Lightning

5. Debris burning
   Examples: burn barrels, rubbish heaps, leaves, slash piles. Avoid burning during the wrong season, leave no fire unattended no matter what time of year it is, and be sure the fire is completely put out when you're through.

6. Campfires
   Examples: fires outside campgrounds, transients, burning without a permit, stacking wood beside the fire, failing to remove forest litter from the campfire area.

7. Playing with fire
   Examples: firecrackers, matches.

8. Electrical power
   Examples: tree limb abrasion, outdoor extension cords. Take responsibility for the power lines near trees at your homesite—don't wait until a fire starts.

9. Smoking
   If you must smoke, do so in an area completely free of flammable materials and be aware of wind that may carry the ash into dry grass or leaves.

10. Railroad

There are many subtle ways a fire can start accidently that most people aren't aware of. For example, if you are in the car and must pull off onto the shoulder to slow or park, your car's exhaust or superheated underside of the engine may come in direct contact with dry grass. This is enough to start a fire, and if you pull back onto the road and drive off, you may leave smoldering embers that will burst into flame. The same can apply when you drive down two-track dirt roads that have dry stubble in between the tire ruts.

Off-road vehicles such as a four-wheel-drive pickup truck or motorcycle can also ignite dry grass from its hot engine or exhaust pipe. A wood cutter's hot chain saw set into dry leaves can easily begin a smoldering ground fire. Landscape tree limbs rubbing on power lines can work through the insulation and spark a fire.

A final source of fires, which occurs frequently in late summer on ranges, is lightning. The clouds rise out of hot lowlands into the mountain forests where there is plenty of fuel and difficult access. These can be dry storms with no drenching rain to put out trees burning from lightning strikes. Smoke Jumpers are dropped by parachute into these remote hot spots to stop the blazes before they become a major wildfire. Today's advanced aerial bombardment firefighting equipment also helps control lightning fires.

The infamous Mann Gulch fire of Montana in 1949 was not unusually large but proved an example of how dangerous lightning fires in the back country can be for firefighters. Sixteen men jumped out of the plane that day, but twelve soon burned to death trying to outrun a blaze that had risen up into a monstrous fire whorl that chased them up a very steep rocky cliff. Only three managed to escape over the top. This and many sad cases include significant losses of personnel and residents. In the face of powerful wildfires, human life becomes powerless. Yet we must continue to live with summer lightning fires and accept them as the natural regime of summer weather in the mountains and wildlands of the west.

4

WATER: YOUR
ESSENTIAL RESOURCE

Water is the single major tool in fighting wildfires. Drive through any Western state from July through November and you'll probably find all but the largest rivers have dried up for the season. Firefighters are also faced with this shortage, forcing ground crews to drive water tender trucks long distances to refill. If firefighters cannot obtain water to defend your home against an oncoming fire, there is little they can do except manually create a fire break. In many fires, the crews are unable to protect every home, choosing only those that can be safely defended. They leave the rest to burn. **Creation of defensible space coupled with an emergency water supply are the two most important factors which determine whether your home can be saved.**

In recent fires it has become clear that there simply is not enough manpower to defend every homesite. There are too many homes now on the fringes of wildlands, a situation taxing even the most effective firefighting teams. Protection of your house may depend largely on forethought and planning to effectively douse spot fires until it is unsafe to continue or the danger ebbs. Water supply is not your only concern. During major wildfires electrical lines and poles often burn to cut off the power supply. Without electricity, you cannot operate a domestic well pump, or any other kind of pump for that matter unless you have a suitable generator. This shows how both water supply and the means to deliver it are equally as important.

Efforts to put out the blazes in San Francisco after the 1906 quake were hindered by the loss of pressure and supply in the city water mains. Even if you are on a municipal system, the pressures needed by firefighters at the hydrants will reduce the overall operating pressure and flow rate, leaving very little for your efforts. Conversely, your demand for water along with that of other residents in your community can combine to reduce pressure needed by firefighters. This pressure loss can happen in any suburb, proving a home water supply independent of any municipal system is the only assurance of successfully fighting your own fire. In addition, this system also allows you to fight a house fire until the volunteer fire department arrives.

Design and installation of an emergency water supply and delivery system can be a complicated matter. There are many variables, such as the amount of water you have available, the distance it must travel to the point of delivery, and the flow rate demands. Flow demands relate to how much water is used over a certain amount of time. Eventually your supply will be exhausted, and the more quickly you draw out the water, the shorter period of time you will be able to protect your home.

If you have not created a defensible space around your house, even the best emergency water system will have little, if any, impact on a full-scale wildfire. The information provided in this chapter is based on homesites that have not only created defensible space, but also maintain it correctly. **Consult with an expert when designing your system to be sure it is adequate and functions as intended.**

EMERGENCY WATER SUPPLIES

Forestry experts recommend that an emergency water reservoir for your home contain at least 2,500 gallons, preferably more. Some rural building departments may require larger storage capacities, especially when very large homes or homesites are concerned. The more water you hold, the longer you are able to fight a fire. The reservoir should be located close to the house where you or the firefighters can gain safe access. A valve to access the water supply should match that of local firefighting agency equipment for increased protection if not stipulated by building codes.

There are many ways to create a reservoir to hold the emergency water supply that range in price and maintenance requirements. It is essential to evaluate purchase price, installation, maintenance, and longevity to be sure you are buying a reliable storage system. Water evaporates very quickly in hot, dry weather, and unless your water supply is fully contained and airtight, it will gradually dwindle away. **An effective emergency supply must be kept consistently full at all times.**

DOMESTIC WELLS Most homesites that are not supplied by a municipal water system rely exclusively on a domestic well. How much water the well produces is rated in gallons per minute, or GPM. In some areas households survive on just 2 GPM, which requires a storage tank reservoir because an indoor sink faucet draws at least 3 GPM. Other people are more fortunate, with wells producing anywhere from 10 to 100 GPM, and they use a small pressure tank to regulate their pumping needs.

Heavily producing wells fed by water-filled underground caverns or rivers can make excellent emergency reservoirs. But most wells are supplied by aquifers, which are deep gravel strata containing water. If a well fed by a slow-moving aquifer is pumped continually for a long period, it may exceed the speed of replenishment and dry up for a time until recharged. This is the problem with relying solely on a well for emergency water supply.

SWIMMING POOLS The most versatile but expensive large water reservoir for a homesite is a swimming pool. A standard size will contain more than enough water for most fire situations. Where the climate is too cool to warrant a swimming pool, spas and hot tubs are viable options, and there are many cases where their water has saved homes. These present the greatest installation cost, but this cost is offset by the recreational use. There is also maintenance to consider, with chemicals and extensive mechanical systems. But a well-maintained pool is relatively free of debris, which can dog and disable your delivery system.

Aboveground vinyl-lined swimming pools such as the "Doughboy" also provide a considerable amount of water for firefighting. These pools are not as long-lived as more traditional swimming pools because the liners tend to deteriorate over the years, and unless replaced may begin to leak. In addition, liners will melt quickly if flames get close. For homesites on sloping or rocky ground it may be difficult to set up one of these pools without extensive grading.

PONDS Ponds are natural water bodies that must be filled periodically since they rely on dense clay soil to retain water. Construction of a pond as fire reservoir should be well thought out before grading begins. Rainfall is not sufficient in some states to keep the pond full, and with a large surface area, evaporation occurs quickly. Be sure you have a reliable, heavily producing spring or well to ensure a consistent water level.

Construction of a functional and successful pond should be supervised by an engineer or contractor. These experts are qualified to evaluate the location, design, and construction of a pond large enough for fire water. The soil must be analyzed for its water-holding capability because porous soil structure, fissures and cracks in bedrock can allow water to leak out unseen. In the case of leaking ponds, there are few solutions— mainly an expensive vinyl lining system. The walls of a pond must be graded properly for safety and to reduce the incidence of the unwanted wetland vegetation that thrives in shallow water. Tules and cattails can eventually fill the entire pond, restricting access to the water or displacing it altogether. In some cases waterfowl will be drawn to the pond, which can create a mess along the banks and reduce water quality. But for those who wish such a wetland ecosystem this may not be a liability.

TANKS Where a swimming pool, productive well, or a pond is not possible, a water tank is the next best choice. Tanks sold today are usually wood or plastic, though some people bury concrete septic tanks which hold about 1,500 gallons of water. This is 1,000 gallons short of the minimum needed and to increase it a second tank is required. The equipment needed to move these heavy containers to their final resting place may be hampered by limited access, and once there septic tanks are so heavy they can't be moved by hand.

Redwood tanks are expensive and difficult to obtain in many areas. Wood tanks resemble hot tubs and consist of a circular base fitted with upright boards for the walls held together with steel bands. Keep in mind a tank of any size can be difficult to set up and is best left to the experts.

A dry redwood tank has gaps between the slats of wood which make up the outside wall. When sufficiently wet the wood expands to close the

Natural ponds are easy to create in low areas for beautiful landscape features that also serve as back-up fire water. Keep a gasoline powered pump and fire hose nearby to fight a structure or wildland fire on-site even if the electricity is shut off.

FIRESCAPING TIP

If you would like the option of taking a dip in your fire water tank, an open-topped model is available. The largest you can transport is six feet deep and ten feet wide. This gives you a ten-foot diameter pool containing 3,500 gallons of water, a sufficient volume that won't heat up during the summer. It should be free-standing and have a double flange at the top. To improve water quality just fill and let it overflow for a while, or add swimming pool chlorine if you can't spare the water. For the redwood tank "look," surround the outside with six-foot-long cedar fence boards and secure them with two or three cables tightened by turnbuckles. Include a circular tarp for the top to keep debris out when not used for swimming.

This is an open-topped, plastic chemical tank measuring 6 feet tall and 10 feet in diameter. Only the white plastic flange around the top is still visible. Cedar fence boards have been added around the outside to give it a redwood look and are held in place by the tension of just three small cables tightened with turn-buckles—none of the liabilities of a wood tank yet every bit of the beauty. This tank will have evaporation and litter if not cleaned out, while a fully enclosed plastic tank will always be ready to deliver.

gaps, thus sealing the tank. From this point on, the tank must be kept full and at a consistent water level to prevent the gaps from reopening when the wood dries and shrinks. If there is no reliable water supply to keep the tank full at all times, slats exposed by low water dry out and leak until refilled and the wood expands again.

Finding a good redwood tank is no easy matter. Most of those which are sold as "used" are snatched up as soon as they become available, either by homeowners or tank resale and construction companies. Even an old tank is expensive, and the price of a newly manufactured one is exorbitant. However, there are no other aboveground tanks that blend into the landscape as beautifully. High cost, limited availability, complicated set-up, and the need for water level consistency are all reasons why redwood tanks are not more widely used.

With the advent of modern plastics there are now excellent heavy duty rigid tanks that make good alternatives to redwood. The plastic tanks are lightweight and simple to move around, although they do not break down into transportable units as with wood tanks. You will find there is a limit to sizes of plastic tanks which can be shipped by truck Those that are cylindrical, say six feet in diameter, but twenty feet long will fit well on a tractor-trailer rig. A wider tank presents problems and may require a step-down trailer or a wide load permit, which will complicate shipping.

You can set up a plastic tank by simply leveling a spot on the ground and spreading a layer of sand evenly upon the surface. Since plastic does not decompose like wood, it can be set directly upon the sand bed and is instantly ready for use. Moving a plastic tank is simple; first empty the contents using a siphon hose, then simply tip on its side and roll across the ground. Most plastic tanks are geared for chemical containment, so they are long-lived, heavy duty, and surprisingly durable.

Plastic tanks are available in a wide variety of shapes and sizes to choose from. Some are fully enclosed upright cylinders with only a small opening at the top for cleaning and filling. Others resemble a gasoline station underground tank, which are large, fully enclosed cylinders that lie horizontally upon the ground. These make exceptional underground cisterns for cold weather country such as Colorado, when fires often erupt in the dry winter weather. A fire hose valve can be installed for you by the manufacturer for easy pump or hose hook up

CISTERNS   A cistern is an underground water storage unit. Due to the excavation costs they tend to occur only on very old homesites or those in affluent neighborhoods where they are used for domestic potable water. The underground insulation makes this the best choice for storage where winters are too cold for above-ground tanks. The advantage of a cistern is that it is located out of sight and not subjected to litter problems of open-water reservoirs. The water is insulated by the earth so it remains at an even temperature.

A lined, underground cistern for *nonpotable* water can be fed all winter by rain gutters, then remain in reserve until fire season. These are enclosed systems with very low evaporation rates. Some people build their cisterns by burying a heavy, plastic tank underground where it is out of site and low enough so that gravity will cause rain gutter downspouts to drain directly into the tank without pumps.

PUMPING FIRE WATER

Even if you have the largest water supply in the Western World, when the electric lines burn and power is cut off, there is no means of pumping the water under pressure. One resident recently faced with an oncoming fire suddenly realized he could not access the 16,000 gallons in his underground cistern because the fire would burn his power lines long before it reached the house. Obtaining power to extract water from your reservoir and pressurize it sufficiently to make a difference is the other half of the emergency water supply equation.

The two basic means of supplying power to run your fire water pump are with a **gasoline electrical generator** or a **gasoline water pump.** The gasoline-powered generator is used to supply power to an electrically operated water pump that may already be in place. A gas water pump is a simpler, more direct means of pulling water out of a reservoir and pressurizing it for fire flows. These portable self-priming pumps are inexpensive, easy to use, and they may be kept safely indoors and out of the weather until needed.

FIRESCAPING TIP

A good way to simplify a domestic well emergency fire system is to build a weather-tight well house or shed over the well head and pressure tank if you have one. Design it so there is a safe place for the generator close enough to the well wiring to make quick connections safe and simple. This eliminates the need to bring the generator out to the well during a fire emergency.

Rodent damage can ruin parts of a pump, hose, or generator. Whenever possible protect or store these items away from chewing pets and pests, and check them frequently for any sign of damage. Keep in mind a single wire chewed by a field mouse could cause the loss of your home.

If your water supply is a domestic well or underground cistern, it is accessed differently than other types of reservoirs. Water can be drawn by a submersible pump suspended by pipe down into the water. It is driven by electrical wires which extend from the power supply at the top of the well head, down the shaft to the pump. These wires then run from the well head to the house electrical breaker panel. Using a generator connected to the breaker will be useless, however, if there is a house fire or if the lines between the panel and your pump are burned. Therefore it's best to provide an alternative power supply as close to the well head as possible. This is usually a gasoline-powered generator set next to the well.

It pays to hire an electrician who can help you select a generator strong enough to easily run a large well pump. He or she will take into consideration the demands of a fire water system and can also help you pick a generator with enough power to run your household during power failures of any kind. During winter storms, power is often lost and rural residents discover they have no access at all to their well water. A portable electrical generator comes in handy for anyone far from town. The electrician will ensure there are no expensive mistakes which may burn out the pump or generator under prolonged use.

When in place, test the generator system a number of times to see that it starts easily and operates properly. This also familiarizes you with the system so you don't run into problems when a critical situation arises. Run the system for an hour or more because if you have not sized your wiring properly, it will heat up to indicate the amperage draw is too high for your connection. The time to discover there is a problem with your system is not during a fire.

To draw and push water out of other types of reservoirs such as tanks, ponds, and swimming pools, a gasoline-powered pump is the simplest method. These pumps vary in size and most are portable. It's a good idea to buy a pump that can be transported to the water source by one person, because there is no assurance a second person will be at home when the fire starts. If it is too heavy for one person to move, construct a weather- and rodent-proof house to store fire equipment close to the water source.

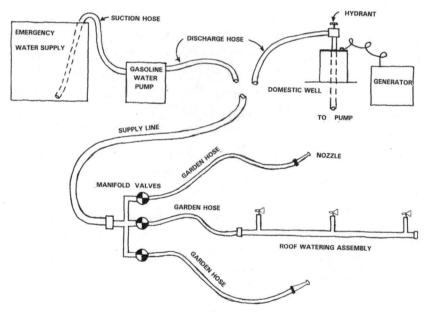

Emergency Water Supply System Diagram

This diagram shows the basic components of a water supply system using either a domestic well or another storage reservoir. This is schematic and does not take into consideration operating pressures or the final sizing of pipe or hose as this can vary considerably depending on the site.

There will be two places for hoses to be attached to the pump. One is the **suction port** that draws water out of the reservoir and through the pump mechanism. The water comes out the other side of the pump under pressure through the **discharge port**. You must have a hose of sufficient size to extend from the suction port to the deepest point in the reservoir to be able to use the entire water supply. The hose attached to the discharge port must be long enough to reach all parts of your house or any fire suppression systems you have devised. The pump should also be **self-priming** so it becomes immediately useable. If your water source is not particularly clean there should be a filter or "suction strainer" at the end of your suction hose so that no debris will enter the system and clog nozzles or sprinklers. Pumps designed to handle light debris are a good way to prevent clogs with an unfiltered water source.

SIZING THE PUMP

Water pumps vary in size, and there is certain criteria that are important to know in order to select a model sufficient for your needs. **Warning: To be sure you are buying the right-sized pump for your emergency fire system, enlist the aid of a professional**. Some counties or cities require a mandatory emergency fire system be installed at each home, and in this case they supply specific criteria for you to follow. The local municipal fire station may be able to send a professional to your home to help design a system. In rural areas state forestry agencies may be able to offer their expertise as well.

FIRESCAPING TIP

You'll find there are two general classes of water pumps. Those which are labeled specifically as fire pumps are more expensive than standard gasoline-powered water pumps. This is because these are used by professional firefighters who demand certain standards. If you can afford one, these are the best and most reliable you can buy.

A registered civil engineer is probably the best resource, but he or she will require payment for consulting time and design services. The cost of a civil engineer is worthwhile when designing larger systems for rural homes, farms, or ranches. Factors such as friction loss must be calculated into a piping plan in order to prevent a loss of pressure over long runs of pipe. You will feel more confident with a pump selected by a professional who has factored in all the variables of your site.

IMPORTANT DEFINITIONS RELATING TO SIZING A PUMP

GALLONS PER MINUTE (GPM)   The amount of water passing a point in the line over a given time. This might also be labeled as velocity of flow, or flow rate. Firefighter's portable pumps used by agencies generally deliver 30 to 35 gallons per minute through a 1½-inch diameter hose. Home systems may put out more than this, with 100 GPM ideal if the reservoir is large enough.

PRESSURE (PSI)   The energy or force of the water at a given point in the line. Expressed as pounds per square inch. Firefighter's portable pumps deliver at about 75 to 90 PSI through a 1½-inch diameter hose.

FRICTION LOSS   The loss of pressure caused by water flowing in the system calculated according to each linear foot of pipe, its diameter, the number and type of fittings, and the gallons per minute.

FEET OF HEAD, HEAD PRESSURE   This is a means of factoring in gravity demands on a pump. One foot of head equals .43 PSI. For example, if your water source is 100 feet below the roof of your house, in order to factor in gravity you will need at least 43 PSI added to standard operating pressures for water to reach the roof under adequate PSI. However, this must also be combined with friction loss as well. This illustrates how technical sizing of pumps, hoses, and piping layout can become on a large-scale system. It is suggested that an engineer or other qualified professional be enlisted to design or check your system components before you select a pump.

HORSEPOWER   This is the way small gasoline engines are sized. The greater the horsepower, the more GPM the pump will push. This also relates to PSI with larger engines needed for high pressure systems.

ELECTRIC START PUMP   Gasoline engines are usually fired up manually with a recoil start. More sophisticated models are available with push-button starting systems, which require a battery. Battery maintenance is critical to their reliability over the long term, so it may be wise to have a recoil start as well for backup.

DELIVERING FIRE WATER

Your water source will be the discharge port on your pump. The hose or its coupler must be the same diameter as the port which usually ranges from 1 to 2 inches, but this does vary with each pump. Many pumps are rigged for a "lug coupler," which is a special brass fitting preferred for larger diameter connections and used by firefighters. If your hose is smaller than the discharge port, you can attach reducing bushings to decrease the size.

Garden hose diameters range from ½ to ¾ inch, which is relatively small in firefighting terms. They are also made of rubber and other materials that may melt easily in the event of a fire. For the most reliable system, it is recommended your main supply hose be a 1½-inch standard cotton-jacket fire hose designated for outdoor fires. Avoid hoses designed for use inside buildings such as those stored permanently in hallways of offices and hotels.

This large fire hose can extend from your reservoir to the house. You can attach a variable firefighting nozzle, which is valuable if you must fight a house fire and need maximum delivery. But for wildfires, you must make a manifold that will split a single large diameter supply line into two or more smaller lines. This is why it is a good idea for the supply line to be as big as possible, because a smaller hose will not deliver very much water if split into multiple-delivery garden hoses. For example, if the main supply hose was ¾ inch and capable of delivering no more than 10 GPM, that would barely be enough for a sprinkler and a second hand-held hose..

It is best to use a main supply line of the same diameter as your discharge port, then construct a PVC or galvanized iron manifold that splits into three or four different lines. Iron tends to last longer than PVC but is prone to rusting. Attach a ¾-inch or larger gate valve to each port on the manifold and buy a high-quality garden hose for each one. Also have variable brass nozzles on hand so that you can change from a long stream

FIRESCAPING TIP

1. **Foam Systems** There are more sophisticated home wildfire systems available which rely on fire-retardant, nontoxic chemical foam products. These are permanent roof systems that may be activated automatically to apply a layer of fire-retardant foam over the roof and exterior walls of your home. The problem with foam in the past is its longevity, both in a stored state and after it is applied to your house. Some smaller companies are developing a portable foam system which many feel shows great promise but may not be widely available nor proven. To find out about contractors carrying these systems and related products contact your nearest fire station or firefighting agency.

2. **Fire Hose Care** Cotton-jacket fire hoses are vulnerable to mildew and rot if not stored properly. If you visited a wildfire site where cleanup is in progress, you'll find the firefighter's hoses stretched out in the sun to dry. It is important to dry your own hose out **completely** before you roll it up. Lay it out on your driveway or another dry surface, let it dry awhile, then roll it over so the underside dries too. If you don't dry it thoroughly, the cotton will soon rot right off the rubber core, and because the wet cotton acts as insulation, half the value of the hose will be lost. Note the degree of dampness or moisture accumulation where you plan to store your hose to avoid problems.

spray to mist with a simple adjustment, or even turn it off entirely without going back to the valve. This assembly allows you maximum control at both the gate valve and the brass nozzle. It is important to discuss your manifold with a fire system consultant. Each time the supply line splits there will be a reduction in GPM as well as pressure. If there is no compensation for this at the pump or main supply line you may end up with an anemic flow. **The more water you demand of the system, the faster your reservoir will be depleted.**

ROOF WATERING SYSTEM

During a fire where embers are falling like rain, you can't be everywhere at once. It may surprise you how much area there is to cover on the average roof and how quickly the water evaporates from the surface of roofing materials. The best way to keep it consistently moist is to use sprinklers. If you were to set up individual sprinklers you'd need a separate hose for each one. The best way to resolve this is to make your own miniature sprinkler system which is designed to fit the contours of your roof.

The easiest way to cover a roof is to supply water at the ridgeline so it may run down both sides evenly. Spray sprinklers such as impact heads will lose a lot of water to evaporation as it flies through the air, particularly in the heat of an oncoming fire. One alternative is the soaker hose which has tiny holes pricked all along its length. Lie one of these on each side of the ridgeline and there will be less evaporation and better saturation of the entire roof surface. Other products such as leaky pipe and some new alternatives are worth investigating, but they must be able to hold up over the years in storage without breaking down.

This is not to say spray heads are taboo. A basic ½- or ¾-inch PVC plastic-pipe with two or three risers topped with sprinklers can be easily made at home. Add a sprinkler hose coupler to one end of the supply line and cap off the other. This gives you plenty of coverage if placed atop the ridgeline. If you have a manifold on your supply line you can set up these sprinklers and then be free to travel around the house to put out embers and spot fires with another hose line.

5

CONCEPTS USED IN FIRE-RESISTANT LANDSCAPES: MANAGING NATIVE VEGETATION

The wildland-urban interface is a term coined to describe the increasing exposure of homesites to the threat of wildland fires. Until 2017 this was a clearly defined transition zone, but after Santa Rosa's safe neighborhood burned so unexpectedly, the concept is evolving further. Think carefully about overall vulnerability before purchasing a house. Pause and consider the surroundings of your current house, and then decide if there is anything you can do to reduce the risk to your own property or that of the entire community.

The **classic interface** involves homes and subdivisions growing around the edges of cities where younger families prefer to live. Most commute to work. These areas may appear more secure from fire threat than they actually are. Paved streets and fire hydrants, along with extensive landscaping, all project a suburban character, yet as the crow flies these homes may be surprisingly close to high-fuel-volume wildlands.

The **mixed interface** consists of more scattered developments, smaller subdivisions with larger parcel sizes. Ranchettes, vacation homes, and single isolated homesites can be completely surrounded by extensive wildlands. Those who choose this lifestyle are interested in preservation of the natural environment, wildlife, and native vegetation. Although foresters and land managers suggest we must step in and assist in maintaining healthy wildlands, these homeowners are hesitant to disturb "pristine" countryside. Upscale rural planning departments also tend to follow this path. Many county ordinances strictly control or outlaw the removal of trees and other vegetation either for aesthetic reasons or when wildlife agencies deem it habitat. This is the case with Berkeley's giant "heritage" eucalyptus trees, newly considered monuments despite the fact that each one is a conflagration waiting to happen amidst high density neighborhoods around the university. It's an unusual preservation concept after the extreme losses of the Oakland firestorm in 1991, largely driven by an eucalyptus crown fire.

The reality is that even Native Americans altered the landscape hundreds or even thousands of years ago. They migrated with the seasons, their horses distributing seed from one camp to another. With the help of fire and other horticultural techniques native peoples actively managed their land, never allowing it to reach the overgrown, congested state we see today.

In the mixed interface, tremendous fuel volumes can accumulate due to restrictions as mentioned above, and from other side effects of urbanization. For example, vegetation that is disturbed but not removed becomes less healthy and subjected to disease and pests such as the pine bark beetle or oak root fungus. Many native trees do not tolerate disturbance to their root zone and decline if surroundings have been sufficiently altered. Paving, grading, livestock grazing, introduction of irrigation water, and changes to groundwater levels all contribute to the decline of plant communities in these areas. Many quasi-rural neighborhoods throughout the West are still living in "ignorant bliss" amidst an overgrown, volatile countryside.

The **occluded interface** is more subtle than these first two. It deals with sometimes highly developed urban areas that contain unmanaged open or uncultivated spaces left to build fuel volumes. In 1985 three homeowners died when an eight-acre fire within the Los Angeles metropolitan area swept up a steep slope and overran their homes. Santa Rosa and the Oakland fire are hardly considered rural or even suburban, both losing thousands of homes.

Many unmanaged open spaces in urban areas are a result of undevelopable land such as overly steep slopes. Cut-and-fill subdivisions may have nearly vertical slopes between building pads that are difficult to negotiate and manage. Throughout newer communities these areas are threaded into subdivisions, with some irrigated and landscaped. They tend to be heavily vegetated to reduce soil erosion and can accumulate tremendous amounts of fuel if not regularly pruned. In some cases these areas are considered a natural "open space" amenity to separate clusters of high-density housing. In all of these cases there is a single common denominator: accumulations of vegetation and fuel loads. It is up to the homeowner to manage these areas around his or her homesite because leaving it to association maintenance services, the city, or simply ignoring it all together can be deadly.

In recent years developers planning new housing in areas deemed "wetlands" have been forced by wildlife regulatory agencies to compensate for the loss of habitat by setting aside zones within their projects for reestablishment of new wetlands. Most wetlands, particularly in those in the West, are seasonal, remaining green and moist for only a few months of the year. Unlike a maintained and irrigated public park, these habitat spaces become choked with orchard grasses, reeds, berry vines, and wild grapevines, all ideal cover for wild animals and birds. But during fire season in the late summer and fall this dense vegetation grows dangerously dry, and fires are likely to become a problem. Homes adjacent to these areas are vulnerable to crown fires, with flames traveling quickly throughout the subdivisions via rooftops and landscape tree canopies.

EVERYONE IS AT RISK

The mistake most people make is thinking that because there is a fire hydrant down the street it automatically protects them from wildfire. As illustrated in occluded interface scenarios, this is not always the case. Although a small city lot is easier to keep fire safe, there are still many things you must do to reduce the possibility of flying embers igniting the home.

It is actually the classic and mixed interfaces that are at greatest risk because of the surrounding wildlands and spotty leapfrog development patterns. Concepts for protecting these homes through vegetation management begin with understanding the definition of defensible space. This is simply a band of managed vegetation around a home that slows the movement of fire by denying fuel and provides a space for firefighters to take a stand to protect the house. When entire communities are threatened there may not be enough firefighters or equipment to protect every home. **Firefighters are more likely to take a stand at homes with defensible space than at those which cannot be separated from the surrounding vegetation.** Naturally you will want your house to be one of these chosen few.

CREATING A DEFENSIBLE SPACE

The overall size of your defensible space is based on the topography and limits of your property. The steeper the slope of your homesite, the larger an area is needed for a defensible space. This is because fire travels much more quickly uphill than it does on level ground, and it is difficult for firefighters to access steeper sites. To compensate, a larger area must be controlled.

The minimum area for homes on less than a **20 percent slope** should extend outward 100 feet on every side. If the house is on a **20 to 40 percent slope,** which is fairly steep, you will need to extend 150 feet uphill, 150 feet on each side, and 200 feet downhill. For slopes **over 40 percent,** manage 200 feet uphill, 200 feet on each side, and 400 feet downhill.

Literature on basic homesite clearing is available from most fire protection agencies, but the defensible space concept takes this idea further to create a manageable area that is larger and more attractive. Simply clearing the ground of vegetation does reduce fire hazard, but it also creates an environment for soil erosion. Firescaping the defensible space is the best way to eliminate the erosion potential and improve the visual quality of a homesite.

The defensible space of each homesite is divided into three distinct conditions or bands radiating outward from around the house. Firescaping deals with the management of existing vegetation within the bands and the addition of ornamental plants with fire-resistant qualities or naturally low fuel volumes. The first step is to define the limits of each band at your homesite and then take care of existing vegetation accordingly.

Zone 1 is the first five to ten feet around the outside walls of the house. Combustible materials in this area are close enough to bring the

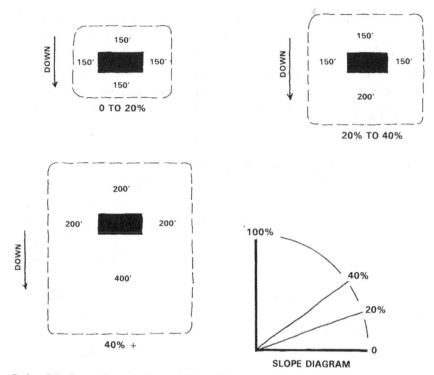

Defensible Space Boundaries and Slope Diagram
The outside limit of defensible space should be measured from the nearest building wall and extends outward from 150 to 400 feet. The required distance increases as slopes become steeper. The down-hill dimension is always larger because this is where fire and heat raging up the slope can be slowed by lack of fuel and hopefully stopped before it reaches the house. The slope diagram shows how steep slopes are that apply to each example.

fire in direct contact with the building wall, deck, or porch. Planting and landscaping is best limited to very succulent groundcovers, gravel mulches, walkways, and green lawns. If you have limited water supply for irrigation, let it be concentrated here.

Zone 2 begins at the perimeter of zone 1 and extends outward about thirty feet. Plants in this zone may be a combination of both native and introduced species. Trees must be widely spaced to prevent crown fires. Shrubs should be low growing and preferably with high moisture content. Groundcovers, lawn, or mowed irrigated pasture are also acceptable. Due

68

FIRESCAPING TIP

If your lot size is small, creation of a defensible space may require management of vegetation on the adjacent property as well as your own. It is illegal to alter or remove vegetation on property you do not own, and if it is done on government lands there may be serious penalties. If you must control vegetation on adjacent property, obtain permission from the owner (preferably written) before starting work. If it is government land, contact the closest state government office to find out which agency has jurisdiction and what laws govern its management.

to the size and open nature of this area, firefighters are likely to take a stand here to defend your home.

Zone 3 includes natural vegetation which has been modified to reduce available fuel volumes. The width of this band extends to the limit of the defensible space required according to topography as described above. The goal is to thin out overcrowded native plants, eliminate ladder fuels, and remove any dead plants or portions of plants that may spread fire. Fire-resistant plants may also be used here to improve visual quality.

REMOVAL AND REDUCTION: MODIFYING NATIVE VEGETATION

Not every homesite threatened by fire will have native vegetation. In many cases the landscape is barren as a result of large-scale grading and new construction. Older, established homesites may be well vegetated with introduced species that have naturalized in our climate or are growing under irrigation. Trees, shrubs, and vines growing without supplemental watering behave very much like our volatile native plant communities and should be treated as such. Species that are highly volatile and should be removed altogether include acacia, eucalyptus, pampas grass, and hopseed bush, to name just a few. See the extended listing in chapter 6. The first goal in creating a defensible space is to selectively remove plants, then prune to reduce fuel volumes of those which remain.

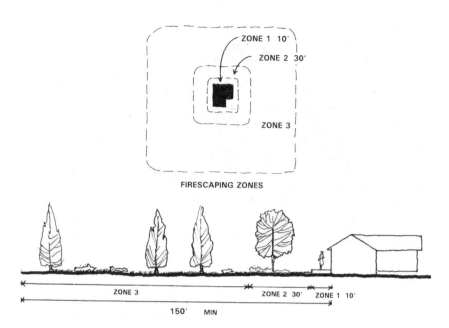

FIRESCAPING ZONES

Plan and Section Views of Fire Band Locations

Fire zones 1 and 2 always remain the same as they radiate first 10 feet then another 30 feet from the walls of the house. If the house has an irregular shape, use the outermost points to begin measuring. The ultimate size of zone 3 can range from 110 feet to as much as 360 feet depending on topography.

Creating a firescape around your home may involve either "remodeling" an existing landscape or the design of an entire landscape from scratch. In either case the same concepts will apply. Some people who have just moved to a rural area have a love affair with native vegetation and the suggestion of removing trees and shrubs is viewed as a mortal sin. But it is important to realize that most wildland areas are unnaturally overgrown due to long-term fire suppression. They are suffering from keen competition for what little soil nutrients and moisture are available. Thinning is actually beneficial and results in much healthier ecosystems.

FIRESCAPING PLANT SPACING GUIDELINES AT A GLANCE

The following guidelines are designed to break the continuity of fuel masses, which will interrupt the horizontal spread of flame from one plant to the other, or vertical movements via ladder fuels.

Trees Minimum from the edge of one tree canopy to the edge of the next one according to topography:
0 to 20% slope = 10 feet
20 to 40% slope = 20 feet
40% and over = 30 feet
Remove all limbs to 15 feet above the ground, but no more than one third of the tree's total height.

Shrubs Zone 2 and 3—spacing is at least five times the height of the shrub.

Warning: If you must remove sizeable trees beware if their trunks are over six inches in diameter at your chest height. These are more safely removed by professionals. Trees are extremely heavy and sometimes unpredictable when they fall, often splintering and breaking into pieces. Consider power and telephone lines, structures, fencing, degree of slope, and wind before attempting to fell a tree. For assistance consult a professional forester for advice, and/or a reputable tree service to do the job safely.

A REVIEW OF IMPORTANT TERMS

SURFACE FIRE Consumes fuels dose to the ground. This can be dead material such as fallen leaves, twigs, and branches, or living fuels such as shrubs, grasses, and tree branches dose to the ground.

CROWN FIRE Travels through tree tops consuming live fuel.

LADDER FUELS Flammable materials occurring between surface fires and crown fires which ad as a ladder to either raise a surface fire to tree crowns, or bring a crown fire down to the surface.

TREE OR SHRUB CANOPY The overall diameter of the foliage head from edge to edge.

MANAGING GRASSLAND

Grasslands cover much of the foothill and prairie ranges of the Western states. They are also the primary vegetation of the Midwestern plains. In the Southern states, the once plentiful savannahs are dwindling. Many of these were once comprised of native grass species but today have been replaced with imported grasses, sedges, and exotic weeds of all sorts. The encroachment of brushlands and sagebrush were once limited by Indian burning, but today without seasonal fires the shrub invasion is more widespread.

Grassland fires were not as serious in the past because there were few ladder fuels to transport flames from the grass to tree canopies. But today the prevalence of various types of shrubs and more plentiful trees have made fires here dangerous. The primary threat in this ecosystem is the spread of grass fires and their ability to move quickly into areas with homes or outbuildings.

The best way to control naturally occurring, unirrigated grasses is by mowing early in the season. If left to go to seed, some species can reach five feet tall with thick, stringy stems. If mowed when long, there will be large amounts of chaff left, either standing or in flammable layers, which

Along the foothills of mountain ranges and the gently rolling landscape of the prairie, grasslands can be mixed with trees to form a woodland.

A fence line and windrow of trees were sufficient for firefighters to stop this grassfire. The gravel road would also have served as a fire break before the flames reached this ranch.

should be raked up and removed. Mowing dry grass with power tools is also a serious fire hazard in itself and is not recommended. If grass is mowed while still green and short, then left to grow a few more inches and mowed once again, the smaller clippings tend to decompose with early season moisture.

The best way to stop a grass fire is to deny it fuel. Because grass fires tend to be of low intensity but fast moving, they can be suppressed more easily by firebreaks. A gravel road or pathway around the house in zone 2 should be sufficient if there are no trees or ladder fuels. It is recommended these barriers be at least five times the height of the uncut grass.

To create defensible space in zones 2 and 3, first remove all dead fuels. This includes lumber piles, unused sheds, standing dead trees, down dead trees, dead shrubs, branches, accumulations of leaves or needles. If there are living vines and shrubs interspersed with the grasses they can act as ladder fuels. Trees should have both live and dead limbs removed from ten to fifteen feet above the ground. Because slopes in this plant community tend to be gradual, each tree should be spaced so there is at least 10 feet between its canopy edge and that of the next tree to check the spread of crown fires. Shrubs should be kept trimmed and thinned to appropriate spacing. Cut away any dead or dying material around the bases.

MANAGING BRUSHLANDS

Brushlands vary considerably across the United States, with each type having its own characteristics. What they all have in common is a greater amount of fuel than grassland, a fuel that produces hotter and taller flames. Burning embers remain viable on the wind far longer than those of grass fires, and can quickly cause spot fires that ignite homes and landscape plants. Some brushlands, such as chaparral of the West, tend to grow in unbroken seas of dense vegetation, creating a fuel-rich avenue through which the fire can travel unchecked. The overall goal in managing these plants is to thin and create trails through, so the continuity is broken up enough to slow the fire and provide an opportunity for firefighters to get around freely.

It is well documented that Southern farmers of the early nineteenth century burned the forests around their farms and homes. They believed it cut down on the insect populations and produced better quality grazing for their livestock. These practices were abandoned with fire suppression in modern times, and, as a result, many Southern states are choking in uncontrolled vegetation. Where the plague of kudzu vines has further complicated this problem, there is an even greater need for mechanically cleaning out brushland and forest.

For many homesites, particularly those in the South where vegetation grows into immense thickets of trees, shrubs, and vines, or in similar conditions along the Pacific Coast, managing such conditions seems an overwhelming task. Some prefer to use heavy equipment to punch through large masses first before doing the hand work, particularly if extensive colonies of poison ivy, oak, or sumac are present. This is understandable as long as there are no downhill water bodies vulnerable to siltation from disturbed soil runoff, and if erosion-control seed mixes are sown the same year. The first step after heavy equipment clearing is to begin thinning the trees and shrubs to appropriate spacing. Remove all debris created by hand work and heavy equipment.

Begin brushland management by removing all native shrubs in zone 1. In zone 2 retain only low-fuel-volume plants less than eighteen inches tall and space those that are to remain as indicated in chart on page 70. You can also group one to three shrubs together into small "islands" and treat them as a single plant. Cut away ladder fuels in all trees and be sure

74

DISPOSING OF SLASH

When the pioneers first began settling in the upper Midwest lake states, they actively logged the great forests. later, when commercial logging was practiced, great piles of slash remained in the devastated areas. Layers twelve to fifteen feet deep were reported just before a series of devastating fires, among them the October 1871 Wisconsin burn that took hundreds of lives. Most experts agree that the fires wouldn't have been nearly as damaging nor as large had there not been such great accumulations of slash.

Whether you are working brushland or forest ecosystems, there may be considerable amounts of slash, consisting of removed trees, shrubs, leaves, needles, twigs, and branches. Where dozer work has been carried out, there may be huge mounds of stuff. If you can't deal with it right away, it's better to separate the material into widely spaced smaller piles than one or two massive ones. Instruct your dozer operator to do this before he begins working on the site so you won't have to divide the piles afterwards. There are four main ways to dispose of the slash:

1. Use a chipper/shredder and grind the smaller material into useful mulch.
2. Salvage any and all firewood. Although this can be tedious in chaparral areas, this takes advantage of a free resource.
3. Haul it to a landfill. This can be difficult and expensive for large jobs, but if work is done in smaller increments it is manageable.
4. Burn the piles. In rural areas burning is done during the winter, and requires the landowner to obtain a permit from local fire protection authorities. The permit may only be used during certain periods. Some people cover their slash piles with tarps or plastic sheeting to keep them dry in rainy weather until ready to burn. More on agricultural burning in chapter 10.

they are properly spaced. Zone 3 shrubs and trees should be spaced as indicated above. Keep these shrubs trimmed and free of any dead combustible material. If dozers have done some of the clearing, there may be a few latent deaths of plants unable to tolerate the soil disturbance. Remove these as they appear.

MANAGING FOREST

Since the advent of fire suppression, our forests have become unusually thick with saplings filling every small space where there is sufficient

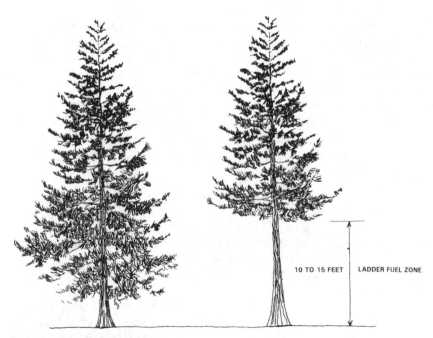

10 TO 15 FEET | LADDER FUEL ZONE

Trimming Ladder Fuels from Trees
The lower branches of trees become the ideal ladder fuel to transport flames from ground level to tree canopies. In ponderosa pines and similar species, the lower branches tend to die but remain attached to the trunk. Tinder-dry, these make excellent kindling and are highly flammable. All dead and living lower branches of every tree should be removed to at least ten to fifteen feet above the ground. If there is a shrub located within the dripline of the tree, the lowest branch should be at least three times as high as the shrub.

FIRESCAPING TIP

1. Plants have a limited life span and a healthy ecosystem is always in a state of transition. New seedlings sprout lo someday make up for the loss of their parent tree, much like people have children to carry on their families. To keep your property healthy and diverse, it's a good idea to select a few of the healthiest baby trees and preserve them within the fire band zones for the future.

2. The thinning of trees to separate the canopies within a firescape should start by removing those individuals which may be unhealthy or display undesirable growth characteristics. Trees with problems could prove short-lived so healthy ones must be given top priority. Closely inspect each one of your trees for the following imperfections:

   Abundance of mistletoe.

   Bark—cankers, blistering, discoloration, splitting, unusual peeling, signs of insect tunnels, large ant colonies, oak balls.

   Damage—girdling, unusual sap accumulations, torn bark, cracking at branch axils, stunted growth, wildlife damage.

   Foliage—premature leaf drop, tip dieback, discoloration, mildew, black residue.

   Form—unusual twisting of trunk, low weak forking, broken top of conifers, leaning, abundant surface rooting.

sunlight. The litter of fallen branches, cones, and thick layers of leaves and needles has accumulated for many decades. Although much of this will eventually decompose, it is being deposited at a much faster rate than decomposition. Conifers and hardwood trees can have ladders of dead branches radiating out from their trunks waiting to transfer flames from a ground fire into the crowns. Dense fields of mountain shrubs completely blanket the ground in some areas. The key to this kind of environment is

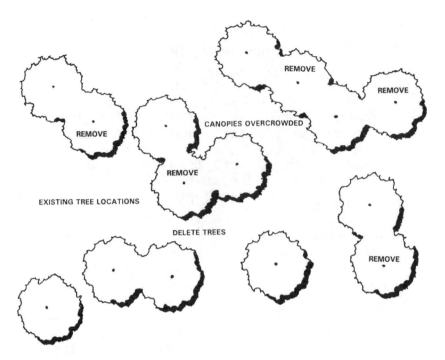

Example of an Existing Tree Layout
Many of these trees have canopies that touch or overlap, which creates an unbroken aerial fuel mass. Some trees will have to be removed so that each one stands alone, and is spaced the appropriate distance from the next tree, and that span depends on slope.

to thin the plants, clean up the ground, and discourage any new seedlings or stump sprouts.

Because many forest land residences are located in national forests or similar protected areas, cutting trees over a certain diameter may be prohibited. **Check with your local government to see if tree cutting permits are required before thinning the forest on your site.** Remove all dead trees whether standing, leaning, or down. On large sites leave one or two dead trees per acre for habitat, but remove all the side branches. Thin remaining trees to appropriate spacing and remove ladder fuels to 15 feet

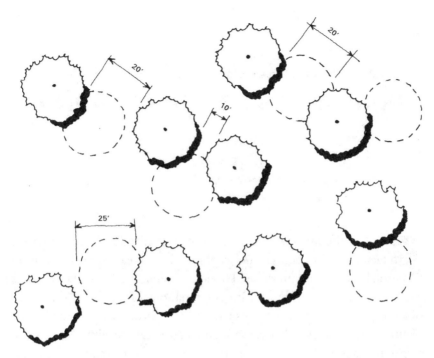

Tree Removal Diagram
The first trees to be removed should always be those weakened by damage or disease. Of those that remain, remove trees that would render the spacings at the appropriate distances. You don't want to take out any more trees than is necessary because they contribute to soil stabilization, shading, and aesthetic beauty of the landscape.

above the ground. Remove all dead fuels. Thin shrubs to proper spacing to break continuity if possible and keep to eighteen inches tall.

6

ORNAMENTAL PLANTS AND IRRIGATION FOR FIRESCAPING

Some of the worst suburban fires occur on hillside subdivisions. One factor that influences landscapes in these areas is erosion control on both cut and fill slopes. Drought-tolerant, soil-stabilizing plants are widely used in the West with combinations of trees and shrubs. In older neighborhoods these plants will be fully mature with accumulations of litter and dead wood because maintenance can be difficult on steep slopes and is often ignored. When these dense, overgrown slope plantings are desiccated by drought they become highly volatile.

It is essential that everyone be aware of potential soil erosion on slopes. On slopes left bare and thus inflammable, integrity could be compromised, and devastating mud slides are all too common, following most large fires like clockwork. When protective vegetation has been removed by mass grading or fires, slopes just don't hold up when saturated. This was clearly the case when the epic 2018 mudslide occurred in Montecito when rains came the month after the Ojai to Santa Barbara Fire. Communities in the Pacific Northwest, with its prolonged heavy rains, are particularly vulnerable to mud slides. Gradual erosion can pit and furrow the slopes or weaken fill materials beneath the surface, where water seeks irregularities in soil compaction. Therefore, it is a given that any firescape on sloping ground must be concerned with erosion control.

The replacement of vegetation or installation of new plants in a firescape occurs mainly in fire bands 1 and 2, those closest to the house. If there is no existing vegetation in zone 3, then planting must also occur there. Before going into the details of plants suitable for these areas, there are important criteria to be considered.

IRRIGATION: THE GREAT QUALIFIER

The single factor governing volatility of plant material is moisture content. A naturally fire-retardant plant such as iceplant will dry up and become surface fuel if denied enough water for the leaves to retain their succulent nature. The big problem facing residents in the arid West, particularly those who own large homesites, is the availability of water to irrigate their firescape plantings. If mandatory water rationing is imposed on those dependent upon municipal water systems, the entire firescape may be left to die without any irrigation at all. Future droughts are inevitable, so the best we can hope for is to design the firescape so it uses all the water at our disposal in the most efficient manner possible.

Over the last two decades there has been a revolution in the world of irrigation. The traditional spray system of high-volume misting heads is falling by the wayside. These heads are not efficient users of water for the following reasons:

1. A portion of the water evaporates into the air from the mist long before it reaches plants and soil.
2. Wind can blow the spray out of planting areas to reduce coverage and even leave some spots completely dry.
3. Blanket coverage waters areas of soil that do not support plant life except weeds.
4. Heads often deliver water at rates greater than the soil can absorb, which results in wasteful runoff.

Plants for firescaping and erosion control tend to be low-growing, groundcover species. These plants can cover large areas of ground in two ways. First are **creeping shrubs,** which consist of a single plant that grow into very large diameters. Only a few plants may be required to cover a sizeable area, although they may take years to reach mature size. Planting them more densely will reduce this time period, but it is still slow. Examples are matlike manzanita or dwarf Oregon grape. The vast majority of plants on the frost-hardy list that follows are either mounding or creeping shrubs.

81

The second group are **spreading plants,** which are more like typical groundcovers and require many individuals to be planted at spacings from 6 inches to 12 inches apart. These rooted cuttings may strike new roots as they grow and eventually fill in gaps, but the rate of coverage varies with each species and the local climate. In cold winter country, these plants have a short and limited growing season as opposed to southern climates where plants grow year around. The reason it is important to distinguish these two types of groundcover is that each is watered in a different way.

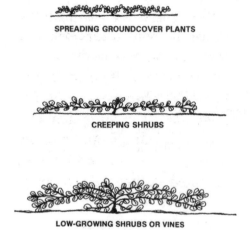

SPREADING GROUNDCOVER PLANTS

CREEPING SHRUBS

LOW-GROWING SHRUBS OR VINES

Variations in Groundcover Plants
Plants with low-growing profiles that spread out to cover large areas of soil can be herbaceous spreaders, creeping shrubs, and vines (which become groundcovers when denied a vertical support). Each is planted, tended, and irrigated in a different way.

The newest techniques in efficient irrigation are drip systems and microspray systems. They both deliver water at such a slow rate their emitters are gauged at gallons per hour (GPH), rather than the gallons per minute (GPM) of traditional spray systems. Drip systems operate under low pressure with the flexible piping either underground, buried beneath mulch or left above ground. Emitters are located at individual plants to wet their root zone and nowhere else. Drip systems tend to concentrate water so it saturates more deeply into the soil and encourages adventurous rooting. The more extensive the root zone, the better able the plant to resist drought.

Microspray heads are just as easy to install because they require the same low pressure piping as a drip system, but use a different type of emitter. Each microspray head actually sprays in a circular pattern with a radius of about 8 to 10 inches. The assembly includes a pencil-like spike that is forced by hand into the ground, but can be pulled up moved around easily because of the flexible supply tubing. The head sits only a few inches above the soil surface so there is less exposure to wind, and a shorter distance to spray, which reduces evaporation. You can easily add or subtract heads as you please because the water demands of each one is minimal.

Each creeping shrub in your firescape may be watered by a drip emitter or microspray head(s). But for spreading plants with sometimes dozens of individuals, it is not always feasible to supply enough drip emitters in such a concentrated area. Microspray heads might serve more than one spreading plant, but over time the entire area may require coverage for the mature stand to remain sufficiently moist and thus fire resistant. This many heads can also make it very difficult and inconvenient to mow herbaceous groundcovers. Keep this in mind when designing your planting plan because without comprehensive irrigation the plants may die or lose their fire-resistant qualities.

If you are faced with a serious water shortage, there is no choice but to design your firescape to work with drip and microspray systems. For best results, the bulk of the area should be planted in large-diameter creeping shrubs and a few widely spaced trees that all can be easily watered by an emitter drip system. To inject more color and interest, smaller zones of spreading plants can be spotted in. Size these zones so each requires from. three to five microspray heads.

LAST RESORT OR WATER HARVESTING

When mandatory water rationing barely allows enough water for bathing and dishes, even a drip system may become too demanding. Under these conditions, which are usually serious droughts, the fire hazard reaches peak levels. To let the firescape wither and die at this time would leave you extremely vulnerable. No matter how much effort is required, do everything you can to preserve the moisture content of these plants.

If you live on the Washington state coastline, it may rain periodically during the summer, but this is a rare occurrence in Nevada or eastern Oregon during fire season. The idea of storing accumulated rain water from downspouts might be a good idea, but some southwestern states do not receive enough rainfall each winter to make it worthwhile. Perhaps further north the possibility increases, but you will need an enclosed storage tank not subject to high levels of evaporation. An underground cistern is ideal but expensive. Fifty-gallon drums are possible, but very heavy when full if they must be moved closer to where water is needed.

Imagine how much water is required to fill your washing machine for a sizeable load. This can range from 15 to 20 gallons, and during a normal cycle it will drain after the wash phase, fill a second time, then drain out again. That is two full drums of water wasted into the sewer. This is why **gray water** utilization, although a nasty term for illegal activity according to most city codes, can mean the difference between a defensible space and a dry, dead, volatile one. The reason it is frowned upon is that harmful bacteria can accumulate if gray water is stored for any length of time. The key is to use it immediately rather than store for later use.

Laundry water is a good source of emergency firescape water because it does not contain grease and food as does dishwater. Laundry is done frequently throughout every season, so there is a constant fresh supply without storage problems. If detergents used are free of dyes and perfumes, the water will contain some nutrients beneficial to plants. However, if water is concentrated and these minerals build up to toxic levels, plants may suffer. When the rinse water is combined with the wash water, the residual detergent is further diluted. In most cases winter rains are enough to flush or leach away the accumulated minerals from the previous year's gray water.

If you remove the washing machine drain hose from your sewer stand pipe and rig it to drain into a barrel outside, you can then ladle out water into buckets to water your plants. You may also be able to devise a siphon system to eliminate the labor of hoisting buckets of water. Firescapes using trees and spreading shrubs are easier to water by this method because you will have fewer individual plants to water, and you can fashion a soil basin around each one to hold the water until it soaks in.

Another source is bathwater, and you can reroute your drain line from the tub or shower as well. In some cases there can be an optional drain so that in the rainy season it drains into the sewer or septic system, then come summer reroute it to water plants. Where this isn't realistic, water can be left in the tub and siphoned out the window through a hose after bathing just as a waterbed is drained.

PLANTS FOR FIRESCAPE BANDS

There are no fireproof plants—they will all burn in an intense fire. But we can select plant species that have an ability to resist fire through unusually high moisture content and those which provide the least amount of fuel to an approaching wildfire. How we arrange and space these plants is also important to interrupt fuel availability. The following are definitions of terms used in this book, which are important to avoid misunderstandings.

FIRE RESISTANT   This is a relative term used to describe plants that are "more resistant" or "less resistant" than other plants. These more resistant plants are made so by higher amounts of moisture within twigs and foliage. Under a low or moderately intense fire, they may be slower to burn, but a really strong fire will char them in a minute. A fire-resistant plant can lose this quality altogether if not properly maintained and irrigated.

LOW FUEL VOLUME   This refers to the amount of fuel an individual plant contributes to an oncoming fire. It relates primarily to size and height. For example, a ground-hugging species of manzanita offers very little if any fuel above 12 inches high for a fire to burn, but an upright inland manzanita species consists of three to five times as much burnable fuel per plant. A naturally low-growing plant allowed to build up dead wood and a mounding habit due to neglect becomes a fire hazard and no longer has a low fuel volume.

Notice how a plant labeled as fire resistant or having a low fuel volume can actually lose these characteristics unless properly maintained. This single concept is pivotal in the long-term effectiveness of a firescape band system.

GROUP I   GREATEST FIRE RESISTANCE

Studies have shown that plant species which retain high levels of moisture in their leaves and stems are the most fire resistant. In every case, these are always succulents. There is some confusion about the fact that succulents have evolved to survive periods of drought by storing moisture in their leaves. This is true, but during these dry times the plants will pucker, wither, and a large portion may die off, depending on the length and severity of the drought. If the succulent is to grow, thicken, and retain its fire-resistant qualities, it must be watered frequently. At the Huntington Botanical Garden in Southern California, the succulents are watered almost every week during the summer months.

The succulents listed as having sufficient fire-resistant qualities for fire bands are primarily iceplants. Like palms, these plants have been long maligned because of their great popularity during the 1960s. It seems as though plants that become trendy can just as quickly be considered tacky and in poor taste. At the turn of the century cacti and succulent gardens were everywhere in Nevada, Arizona, West Texas, New Mexico, and

Virtually any succulent can be added to fire-resistant landscapes because they contain a great deal of water and very little fuel. In a recent San Diego fire, a planting of succulents just like this saved a house.

other dry climates, their unique shapes and intensely colorful flowers considered new and different by immigrants from cold eastern states. Resurrected, iceplants present one of our most promising firescaping groups as water supplies dwindle, because fire-resistant landscape plants that offer such brilliant color are few and far between.

The list of succulent plants accepted as the most fire resistant are comprised of plants with different growth characteristics. Do not assume they are all groundcovers. Some, such as the agaves and aloes, are slow-growing, small plants with tall bloom spikes. Others simply develop into neat, compact

Spaces up against the house can be designed with minimal fuel concepts using gravel and succulents and artistic elements to offer interest in lieu of paving or volatile bushes.

plants. Of course, those which mound or spread will cover the greatest area of bare ground. Iceplant is a generic term given to a vast family of groundcovers comprised of many different genera with varying frost hardiness. Flower color varies as well as leaf size and shape. The chief enemies of all succulents are intense cold, shade, soggy soil, and an overabundance of moisture, which causes stems and leaves to rot.

Those who live in cold winter country may still find hardy species in this list, such as sedums and sempervivums, with frost hardiness that defies logic. Although this list of plants has been tested and widely accepted as our most fire-resistant plants, other less common succulents are no doubt equally capable of resisting flames so long as they are sufficiently watered. Many are easily rooted from cuttings and a single plant can be propagated into a large colony in a fairly short time.

Group I Plant List

Note: Plants listed may show greater or lesser tolerance of frost depending on site.

Botanical Name	Common Name	Form	Degrees F
Aeonium decorum	—	small shrub	25
Aeonium simsii	—	mounding	25
Agave victoriae-reginae	—	small clump	30
Aloe aristata	—	small clump	33
Aloe brevifolia	—	small clump	33
Carpobrontus edulis	Tottentot Fig	groundcover	25
Crassula lactea	—	groundcover	25
Crassula multicava	—	groundcover	25
Crassula tetragona	—	groundcover	25
Delosperma	'Alba' White Trailing Iceplant	groundcover	25
Drosanthemum floribundum	Rosea Iceplant	groundcover	25
Drosanthemum hispidum	Rosea Iceplant	groundcover	25
Lampranthus aurantiacus	Bush Iceplant	groundcover	25
Lampranthus filicaulis	Redondo Creeper	groundcover	25
Lampranthus spectabilis	Trailing Iceplant	groundcover	25
Malephora crocea	Iceplant	groundcover	20
Malephora luteola	Yellow Trailing Iceplant	groundcover	30
Portulacaria afra	Elephant's Food	low shrub	30
Sedum acre	Goldmoss Sedum	groundcover	10
Sedum album	Green Stonecrop	groundcover	25
Sedum confusum	—	groundcover	25
Sedum rubrotinctun	Pork and Beans	mounding	25
Senecio mandraliscae	Blue Iceplant	groundcover	25

Frost Hardy Sedum "Stonecrop" Species	Common Name	Form	USDA Zone
Sedum anglicum	—	groundcover	3
Sedum brevifolium	—	groundcover	3
Sedum lineare (S.sarmentosum)	—	groundcover	3
Sedum spathulifolium	—	groundcover	6
Sedum spurium	—	groundcover	3

GROUP II MODERATE FIRE RESISTANCE

The plants classified in this group are the most fire-resistant, non-succulent species. They are primarily herbaceous, with leaves that retain a high moisture content. This, along with low growing habits, increases fire resistance, but every one of these qualities depends on maintenance.

Many of those in Group II are vigorous groundcovers and vines that display a strong tendency to accumulate dry, dead, woody twigs and stems beneath the actively growing foliage. If these hidden nests of fuel are not removed, homeowners may have a false sense of security as they see only the green leaves and not the tinder-dry fuel underneath. Although salt bush has proven quite fire resistant due to its salt content, it is notorious for building up large mounds of flammable twigs and stems. A prolonged dry period not only reduces moisture content of the foliage, it also stimulates die back, which increases this tendency to accumulate volatile material.

Plants in this group offer us a much wider choice of species to work into a design. Although the prostrate growth habits are a single trait they all have in common, there is great diversity of foliage texture and color. Flower size, color, and season of bloom also varies so that the landscape may provide interest year around. Most plants are widely used in landscaping and easily recognizable. Pay close attention to their frost tolerances because ivy geranium, for example, is a summer annual and may only be permanent in warmest zones.

FIRESCAPING TIP

Iceplant common names often include the descriptive term "trailing." These can be encouraged to cascade off retaining walls, over boulders, railroad ties, and even hang off nearly vertical cliffs if they are given a good planting area at the top. Few, however, are able to gain a foothold on slopes over 30 percent. Rely upon them to protect the soil surface from mild erosion, but their root systems are not extensive enough to prevent large-scale slope failures.

Drought resistant creeping rosemary, *Rosmarinus officinalis 'prostratus'* is an ideal plant for firescaping. It is a culinary herb producing a mat of fine, green leaves and beautiful blue spring flowers.

Since it takes a large number of plants to fill in a sizeable groundcover patch, the most inexpensive means of purchasing them is in flats. The flat is a tray in which a large number of rooted cuttings are grown. You will pay a single price for the entire flat. Some nurseries sell these same plants singly in liners or one-gallon pots. Since a one-gallon plant costs up to five dollars to buy, you are basically paying that price per plant. If a flat costing twelve dollars contains 40 small-rooted cuttings of the same species, it's easy to see the savings with flatted plants. If your nursery doesn't have flats of the plant you are looking for, ask them to special order them for you.

One fault of some groundcovers is that they tend to mature and fill in the spaces, then die out in spots as the stems become woody and cease to produce new foliage at the previous rate. *Osteospermum,* the trailing South African daisy, was once the darling of freeway landscapers, but

HERBS FOR FIRESCAPING

There are some plants in groups II and III that are classified as herbs. Some are culinary while others are suitable for crafts, potpourri, and interior decorating, thus adding a new dimension to firescaping concepts. This bonus provides an excuse to frequently harvest the herbal foliage because plants in firescaping bands must be trimmed and thinned out frequently.

Group II herbs:

Achillea tomentosa—Wooly Yarrow
Artemisia caucasica—Caucasian Sagebrush
Salvia sonomensis—Creeping Sage
Santolina chamaecyparissus—lavender-cotton
Thymus serphyllum—Mother of Thyme

Group III herb:

Rosmarinus officinalis prostratus—Dwarf Rosemary

it was abandoned after early stands began to display this die-out tendency. Other plants that have a tendency to suffer from this aging problem include trailing gazania and ivy geranium. Many new forms of these plants are now on the market that offer more dense habit, wider flower range, adaptation to mowing, and drought resistance.

Many of these Group II plants can be established on steep slopes averaging about 30 to 60 percent, but not all root very deeply. Those most reliable and suitable for erosion control are: *Euonymus fortunei radicans, Myoporum parvifolium prostrata, Vinca major,* and *Vinca minor.*

Irrigation for these spreading perennial groundcovers should be a major concern so they do not become over-dry and lose their fire-resistant qualities. Ideally this should be done by blanket coverage of a standard spray irrigation system if you have a reliable and extensive water supply. But highly efficient low-pressure systems are more realistic for homes dependent on municipal water supplies. These are the types of plants that have many individuals so that typical drip systems are not

A new popular form of the African daisy breeding are the Arctotis hybrids. These have now replaced many of the older freeway daisies with more sophisticated, long lived and vividly colored alternatives.

feasible. A large number of microspray heads can be used, but they get in the way and make it difficult to mow. In cold winter areas the spray system may be set up in spring after mowing, then put away as autumn approaches.

New irrigation products are being developed all the time. If you plan to take full advantage of the colorful flowers and foliage variety of these perennial groundcovers to spice up your firescape, it's best to consult an irrigation expert. He or she will be able to explain the most recent technology and products for efficient water delivery. This is even more important when you are planting slopes that require erosion control. Water behaves differently on sloping ground, and an irrigation designer knows how to compensate for the problems of rapid runoff and slow water absorption into the soil.

GROUP II PLANT LIST

Plants with Moderate Fire Resistance

Botanical Name	Common Name	Exposure	Color	Growth Habit	Comments
Achillea tomentosa	Wooly Yarrow	Sun	Yellow	Mat	Spacing: 6–12" Hardy to 20 F Mow after bloom Zones 3–10
Ajuga reptans	Carpet Bugle	Shade	Blue	Mat	Spacing: 6–12" Hardy to 0 F with dieback Mow after bloom Zones 4–10
Arctotheca calendula	Cape Weed	Sun	Yellow	Mat	Spacing: 12–18" Frost tender Rapid growth Drought tolerant Erosion control Mowable Resprouts Zones 8–10
Artemisia caucasica	Caucasian Sagebrush	Sun	Cream	Mounding	Spacing: 24" Hardy to 10 F Drought tolerant Aromatic Zones 5-9
Atriplex cuneata	—	Sun	None	Mounding	Spacing: 30" Hardy to 20 F Drought and salt tolerant Erosion control Zones 8-10
Atriplex gardneri	Gardner's Saltbush	Sun	None	Mounding	Spacing: 36" Hardy to 20 F Drought and salt tolerant Erosion control Zones 8-10
Atriplex semibaccata	Creeping Australian Saltbush	Sun	None	Mounding	Spacing: 36–50" Hardy to 25 F Drought and salt tolerant Small red fruits Resprouts Zones 8-10

Botanical Name	Common Name	Exposure	Color	Growth Habit	Comments
Ceraslium lomentosum	Snow in Summer	Sun	White	Small spreading	Spacing: 18–24" Hardy to 20 F Short-lived Zones 4-10
Euonymus fortunei radicans	Wintercreeper	Any	None	Spreading	Spacing: 30" Hardy below 0 F Fall foliage color Durable Zones 5–9
Fragaria chiloensis	Wild Strawberry	Part Shade	White	Spreading	Spacing: 12–18" Hardy to 20 F Fast growth Mowable Full sun on coast Zones 4-8
Gazania leucolaena	Trailing Gazania	Sun	Yellow	Spreading	Spacing: 18–24" Hardy to 25 F± Fast growth Drought tolerant Invasive Zones 9-10
Lonicera japonica 'Halliana'	Hall's Honeysuckle	Sun	Yellow/ white	Vine	Spacing: 36" + Hardy to 0 F Fast growth Fragrant Erosion control Zones 4–10
Myoporum parvifolium prostrata	—	Sun	White	Spreading	Spacing: 36" Hardy to 25 F Fast growth Drought and salt tolerant Zones 9–10
Osteospermum fruticosum	South African Daisy	Sun	White/ pur- ple	Spreading	Spacing: 24" Hardy to 25 F Fast growth Erosion control Patchy dieout Resprouts Zones 9–10
Pelargonium peltatum	Ivy Geranium	Sun	Many	Spreading	Spacing: 15–18" Frost tender 30 F Fast growth Zone 10

Botanical Name	Common Name	Exposure	Color	Growth Habit	Comments
Phyla nodiflora	—	Sun	Lilac	Mat	Spacing: 12–15" Frost tender Fast growth Heat tolerant
Potentilla verna	Spring Cinquefoil	Sun/Part Shade	Yellow	Mat	Spacing: 12" Hardy to 5 F Zones 3–10
Salvia sonomensis	Creeping Sage	Sun	Blue	Spreading mat	Spacing: 24" Hardy to 0 F Drought tolerant Aromatic Resprouts Zones 6–10
Santolina chamaecyparissus	Lavender-cotton	Sun	Yellow	Mounds	Spacing: 30" Hardy to 15 F Drought tolerant Aromatic Zones 6–10
Santolina virens	Green lavender-cotton	Sun	Yellow/green	Mounds	Spacing: 30" Hardy to 15 F Drought tolerant Aromatic Fast growing Resprouts Zones 6–10
Thymus praecox arcticus	Mother of Thyme	Sun	Mauve	Mat	Spacing: 6–12" Hardy to 20 F Aromatic Zones 4–10
Thymus pseudolanuginosus	Wooly Thyme	Sun	Light pink	Mat	Spacing: 6–12" Hardy to 25 F Aromatic Zones 4–10
Verbena peruviana	Peruvian Verbena	Sun	Red	Spreading	Spacing: 12–24" Hardy to 10 F Fast growing Mowable Zones 5-10
Vinca major	Periwinkle	Sun/shade	Blue	Spreading	Spacing: 18–24" Hardy to 0 F Fast growing Erosion control Mowable Resprouts Zones 5–10

Botanical Name	Common Name	Exposure	Color	Growth Habit	Comments
Vinca minor	Dwarf Periwinkle	Part Shade	Blue	Spreading	Spacing: 12–18" Hardy to 0 F Fast growing Erosion control Mowable Resprouts Zones 5–10

Notes:

1. All spacings are measured from the center of one plant to the center of the next.
2. Plant height indicators: mat=lowest 0–6" spreading=intermediate 6–12" mounding=shrublike 12–18".
3. "Hardy to" temperatures indicate foliage damage to unprotected plants. Climate zone designations per USDA Plant Hardiness Zone Map assume adequate winter protection. Consult with nursery personnel for local hardiness of plants with "Zone X."

FROST-HARDY PLANTS IN ADDITION TO GROUPS II AND III

Because Southern California has consistently suffered from wildfires, it was the Los Angeles State and County Arboretum that conducted fire-resistance testing on ornamental plants. They tested a relatively small number of the species most commonly seen in that region. This left the vast majority of plant materials untested, particularly those hardy species which are the mainstay of northern gardens.

In order to present a diverse palette of low-growing shrubs and groundcovers for the cold winter areas, we cannot rely on fire-resistance test results but must fall back upon the concept of low-fuel-volume plants. The conifers, which are technically more flammable due to their oil content, are some of the most hardy of all low growers. When creating firescapes in cold climates, we must compromise and include the most ground-hugging varieties of conifers, namely the juniper clan. If arranged properly in small separated islands that interrupt the continual supply of ground fuels, we can compensate for the lack of true fire resistance.

MOWABLE GROUNDCOVERS IN GROUPS II AND III

Some of the groundcover plants in these lists are described as mow-able. This means you can renew the stand by mowing with a rotary lawn mower set at the highest setting. For very steep, rocky, or irregular surfaces, use a string trimmer. It is important the clippings be removed either with a catcher, or by raking after cutting. If left behind they will dry out and become dangerous fuel. In warm winter states, certain groundcovers can be mowed either after blooming or during late winter. Mowing is a good way to get rid of any frost-deadened or discolored leaves and stems. It also helps to remove stems that have become overly woody so that new, succulent ones will grow and support a greater abundance of healthy leaves and flowers. For many gardeners mowing is the easiest way to remove all the faded flowers of matlike groundcovers like cape weed. Some of the best candidates for mowing are hypericum and dwarf vinca.

Landscapers use creeping Verbena and lantana hybrids for vibrant, fast-growing color to fill in gaps between young, newly planted shrubs. If planted as early as possible in spring, the plants will flower prolifically before frost in all but the coldest climates. Where able to winter-over, this groundcover is best mowed after flowers have turned brown.

USDA PLANT HARDINESS ZONE MAP DESIGNATIONS

All temperatures are expressed in degrees Fahrenheit.

Zone 1	Below -50
Zone 2	-50 to -40
Zone 3	-40 to -30
Zone 4	-30 to -20
Zone 5	-20 to -10
Zone 6	-10 to 0
Zone 7	0 to 10
Zone 8	10 to 20
Zone 9	20 to 30
Zone 10	30 to 40
Zone 11	Above 40

The following plant list provides species which can fall into either Group II (II) or Group III (III) depending on the height. Group II plants are naturally lower growing, but, as with all plants, we can carefully prune and shape them to reduce size.

Frost-Hardy Plants for Groups II and III

Botanical Name	Common Name	Size	Zone	Comments
Abies koreana (III)	Prostrate Korean Fir	2' tall, 10' wide	5	Conifer
Aronia melanocarpa (III)	Black Chokeberry	20" tall, 3' wide	4	Deciduous broadleaf White flowers Purple Berries Red fall color
Berberis buxifolia 'Nana' (II)	Box-Leaf Barberry	18" tall, 2' wide	5	Evergreen broadleaf
Berberis thunbergii (III)	Crimson Pygmy Barberry	2' tall, 2' wide	4	'Crimson Pygmy' Evergreen broadleaf Bronze foliage

98

Botanical Name	Common Name	Size	Zone	Comments
Ceanothus x pallidus (III)	Pallidus Ceanothus	2' tall, 4' wide	6	'Marie Simon' Evergreen broadleaf Blue flowers
Chamaecyparis obtusa (III)	Dwarf Hinoki False Cypress	2' tall, 2' wide	5	'Nana Lutea' Conifer
Chamaecyparis pisifera (III)	—	2' tall, 2' wide	5	'Plumosa Compressa' Conifer

Cotoneasters

Botanical Name	Common Name	Size	Zone	Comments
Cotoneaster adpressus (III) *praecox*	Early Cotoneaster	2' tall, 6' wide	5	Deciduous broadleaf Red berries Red fall color
Cotoneaster apiculatus (II)	Dwarf Cranberry Cotoneaster	18" tall, 4' wide	5	'Nanus' Evergreen/ Deciduous Red berries
Cotoneaster dammeri (II)	Bearberry Cotoneaster	12" tall, 10' wide	5	Broadleaf evergreen Red berries
Cotoneaster dammeri (II)	Coral Beauty Cotoneaster	12" tall, 10' wide	5	'Coral Beauty' Broadleaf evergreen Coral pink berries
Cotoneaster dammeri (II)	Lowfast Cotoneaster	12" tall, 10' wide	5	'Lowfast' Broadleaf evergreen Bright red berries
Cotoneaster dammeri (II)	Moon Creeper Cotoneaster	12" tall, 10' wide	5	'Moon Creeper' Broadleaf evergreen Red berries
Cytissus decumbens (III)	Creeping Broom	18" toll, 4' wide	6	Evergreen Yellow flowers spring
Daphne cneorum (II)	Garland Daphne	6" tall, 3' wide	5	'Ruby Glow' Broadleaf evergreen Pink Flowers

Botanical Name	Common Name	Size	Zone	Comments
Erica x darleyensis (III)	Ghost Hills Heath	20" tall, 2' wide	6	'Ghost Hills' Broadleaf evergreen Rose pink flowers
Euonymus obovata (II)	Running Burning Bush	6" tall, 5' wide	4	Deciduous broadleaf Red fruit Native eastern US
Gaultheria procumbens (II)	Wintergreen	6" tall, 3' wide	4	Evergreen broadleaf While flowers Aromatic foliage Red fruits
Gaultheria shallon (II)	Salal	12" tall, 3' wide	6	Evergreen broadleaf Black berries
Helianthemum nummularium (II)	Sunrose	18" tall, 3' wide	5	Many different hybrids Drought tolerant Varying flower color Evergreen

Hollies

Botanical Name	Common Name	Size	Zone	Comments
Ilex cornuta 'Berries Jubilee' (III)	Berries Jubilee Chinese Holly	30" tall, 4' wide	6	Evergreen broadleaf Red berries
Ilex cornuta 'Carissa' (III)	Carissa Chinese Holly	2' tall, 3' wide	6	Evergreen broadleaf
Ilex crenata 'Green Island' (III)	Green Island Japanese Holly	2' tall, 3' wide	6	Evergreen broadleaf
Ilex vomitoria 'Nana' (III)	Dwarf Yaupon Holly	18" tall, 3' wide	7	Evergreen broadleaf Drought tolerant

Junipers

Botanical Name	Common Name	Size	Zone	Comments
Juniperus horizontalis (II)	Bar Harbor Juniper	12" tall, 10' wide	3	'Bar Harbor' Conifer Silver-blue Bronze fall color

Botanical Name	Common Name	Size	Zone	Comments
Juniperus horizontalis (III)	Compact Andorra Juniper	18" tall, 10' wide	2	'Plumosa Compacta' Conifer Gray-green Bronze fall color
Juniperus horizontalis (II)	Prince of Wales Juniper	8" high, 8' wide	3	'Prince of Wales' Conifer
Juniperus horizontalis (II)	Yukon Belle Juniper	6" high, 10' wide	2	'Yukon Belle' Conifer Silver-blue
Juniperus sabina (III)	Arcadia Juniper	18" tall, 4' wide	3	'Arcadia' Conifer Bright green foliage
Juniperus sabina (II)	Broadmoor Juniper	12" tall, 8' wide	3	'Broadmoor' Conifer Feathery bright green
Mahonia repens (II)	Dwarf Oregon Grape	12" tall, 3' wide	4	Broadleaf evergreen Western native Bronze fall color Yellow Flowers
Pachysandra terminalis (II)	Japanese Spurge	10" tall groundcover	4	Broadleaf herbaceous Shade tolerant Mowable
Picea abies (III)	—	18" tall, 8' wide	3	'Pendula' Conifer Weeping habit
Picea abies (III)	—	2' tall, 3' wide	3	'Pygmaea' Conifer Dark green foliage

Hardy Rose Species

Botanical Name	Common Name	Size	Zone	Comments
Rosa carolina (III)	Carolina Rose	2–3' tall	5	US native species Spreading Pink flowers Red fruit Groundcover rose

Botanical Name	Common Name	Size	Zone	Comments
Rosa nitida (III)	Shining Rose	2' tall, Spreading	4	US native species Pink flowers Red fruit Red fall color Groundcover rose
Rosa spinosissima (III)	Scotch Rose	2'–3' tall, Spreading	4	Many varieties Pink, White, or yellow flowers Groundcover rose
Rosa wichuriana (III)	Memorial Rose	2' tall, Flat-spreading	5	Latest species to bloom White flowers

GROUP III LOWER FIRE RESISTANCE

Most of the plants in this list are low-growing woody shrubs, which include many native species. Their leaves tend to be leathery and dry; naturally reluctant to give up moisture under extreme heat or drought conditions. This characteristic makes them equally as unwilling to lose their hoarded moisture under the dehydrating temperatures of an oncoming fire. The plant's natural, prostrate habits also leave very little fuel volume to feed the flames.

Among these species are some of the best drought-tolerant native plants grown today. They are both attractive and durable, yet gardeners everywhere struggle to keep them healthy. Like most of the arid Western native shrubs, they expect long, hot, dry summers with little water, followed by a rainy, wet winter when they do much of their growing. In the heat of summer, plants survive by slowing down their water needs and becoming partially dormant. Watering during summer should be restricted to infrequent but deep irrigations, much like an occasional summer thunderstorm cloudburst.

The chief enemy of many native species is poor drainage and wet roots. This is not a common problem on slopes, so plants growing there will need more water during the spring, summer, and fall. On flat, soggy or very low ground, beware of when and how much water is applied. Manzanita and ceanothus are both notoriously finicky about water out of season or poor drainage in general, so plant them with care.

Baccharis, the coyote bush, has been planted extensively on freeway embankments—similar to many of the inhospitable environments of rural brushland or forest environments. There this plant displays a typical characteristic of creeping shrubs as they age. Because the plant is supported by a stubby, upright woody stem that radiates out with branches in different directions, there is great tension upon this central point, called the crown. When the plant gets old, the main branches that have developed into large limbs of foliage pull away from the crown. If they do not break off (these plants tend to be brittle), their foliage falls away to expose the crown. Direct summer sun upon this central stem causes it to dry and eventually split apart, which signals a decline in the lifespan of the plant. On those freeway plantings you'll see this splitting apart, and if you look closely there's a good view of dense, twiggy growth underneath. Instead of moaning about the rush hour traffic, study the freeway embankment plantings. There you will not only see what grows well in your immediate area, you'll see how coyote bush, African daisy, and a variety of low-growing hardy shrubs behave over the long-term.

FIRESCAPING TIP

It's best to plant most of these species during the fall and not in spring. Fall is when natives are gearing up for their growing season, so transplants will be active enough to resist transplant shock, and ore assured a long, cool growing season to become established. This allows the plant to send its roots out of the pot-shaped root ball and into native soil. When the heat and dryness of summer approaches, these autumn children are more likely to find deeply trapped moisture. To save yourself lots of money and dead, highly stressed plants, plant your firescape in the fall.

You can discourage this weight and splitting of creeping shrubs by judicious pruning beginning with the first year. The goal is to balance the plant and discourage one branch from growing on top of another. The top branch uses the bottom one as a support, denying it light and causing defoliation. Meanwhile the top branch is growing beautifully, gaining new leaves every day to make it heavier. Eventually the bottom branch breaks or collapses from the weight. The top branch never developed a strong stem due to the natural support, so when burdened with its own weight it falls outward away from the crown to expose it. If there is enough weight, this heavy branch will pull against that of branches on the opposite side of the crown and split the plant in half. Visualize this scenario whenever you are pruning to maintain the health and fire-resistant qualities of these creeping shrubs.

Group III Plant List

Plants with Low Fire Resistance

Botanical Name	Common Name	Exposure	Flowers	Growth Habit	Comments
Arctostaphylos hookeri 'Monterey Carpel'	Monterey Manzanita	Sun	Pink	Creeping shrub	Spacing: 3' Hardy to 15 F Drought tolerant Slow growing
Arctostaphylos uva-ursi	Bearberry	Sun	Pink	Creeping shrub	Spacing: 3' Hardy to 20 F± Drought tolerant Slow growing Red berries Zones 3–10
Arctostaphylos uva-ursi 'Point Reyes'	Point Reyes Manzanita	Sun	Pink	Creeping shrub	Spacing: 3' Hardy to 20 F± Drought tolerant Slow growing
Baccharis pilularis prostrata	Dwarf Coyote Bush	Sun	None	Mounding shrub	Spacing: 30" Hardy to 10 F Drought tolerant Erosion control Zones 8–10

Botanical Name	Common Name	Exposure	Flowers	Growth Habit	Comments
Baccharis pilularis 'Twin Peaks'	Coyote Bush Hybrid	Sun	None	Mounding shrub	Spacing: 30" Hardy to 10 F Drought tolerant Erosion Control Resprouts Zones 8-10
Carissa grandiflora 'Green Carpet'	Natal Plum	Sun	White	Mounding shrub	Spacing: 40" Hardy to 20 F Spines Fragrant flowers Edible red fruit Zone 10
Ceanothus gloriosus	Point Reyes Ceanothus	Sun	Blue	Creeping shrub	Spacing: 4' Hardy to 20 F Drought tolerant Zones 8–10
Ceanothus griseus horizontalis	Carmel Creeper	Sun	Blue	Creeping shrub	Spacing: 5' Hardy to 20 F Drought tolerant Zones 8–10
Ceanothus prostratus	Squaw Carpet	Sun	Blue	Creeping shrub	Spacing: 4' Hardy below 0 F (mountain elevations) Drought tolerant Zones 8-10
Cistus crispus	—	Sun	Violet	Creeping shrub	Spacing: 30" Hardy to 15 F Drought tolerant Erosion control Zones 8–10
Cistus salviifolius	Sageleaf Rockrose	Sun	White	Creeping shrub	Spacing: 40" Hardy to 15 F Drought tolerant Erosion control Zones 8–10
Hedera canariensis	Algerian Ivy	Pt. Sun	None	Spreading	Spacing: 14" Hardy to 20 F Erosion control Mowable Resprouts Zones 8–10

Botanical Name	Common Name	Exposure	Flowers	Growth Habit	Comments
Hedera helix	English Ivy	Pt. Sun	None	Spreading	Spacing: 14" Hardy to below 0 F Erosion control Mowable Zones 5–10
Helianthemum nummularium	Sunrose	Sun	Multi	Mounding perennial	Spacing: 18" Hardy to 20 F Drought tolerant Erosion control Short lived
Hypericum calycinum	Aaron's Beard	Sun	Yellow	Spreading	Spacing: 12" Hardy to 0 F Erosion control Mowable Resprouts Zones 5–10
Lantana montevidensis	Trailing Lantana	Sun	Purple	Spreading	Spacing: 18" Hardy to 30± Mowable Zones 9–10
Rosmarinus officinalis prostratus	Dwarf Rosemary	Sun	Blue	Mounding perennial	Spacing: 18" Hardy to 15 F Drought/wind tolerant Erosion control Culinary Herb Zones 7–10
Teucrium chamaedrys	Germander	Sun	Purple	Mounding perennial	Spacing: 12" Hardy to 0 F Drought tolerant Erosion Control

Garden Qualities of Group I, II, and III Plants

Note: Spp. indicates all species of this genus listed in above groups.

California Natives

Arctostaphylos spp.—Manzanita
Ceanothus spp.—California lilac
Baccharis spp.—Coyote Bush
Salvia sonomensis—Creeping Sage

Masses of Flower Color

Achillea tomentosa—Wooly Yarrow
Arctotheca calendula—Cape Weed
Arctotis hybrids—Cape Daisy
Ceanothus spp.—California lilac
Cerastium tomentosum—Snow in Summer
Gazania leucolaena—T railing Gazania
Hypericum calycinurn—Aaron' s Beard
Lantana montevidensis—Trailing Lantana
Malephora luteola—Yellow Trailing Iceplant
Osteospermum fruticosum—South African Daisy
Pelargonium peltatum—Ivy Geranium
Verbena peruviana—Peruvian Verbena
Iceplants: *Carpobrotus, Delosperma, Drosanthemum* spp., *Lampranthus* spp.,
  Malephora spp.

Erosion Control

Arctotheca calendula—Cape Weed
Baccharis spp.—Coyote Bush
Hedera spp.—Ivy
Rosmarinus officinalis 'Prostratus'—Creeping Rosemary
Atriplex spp.—Saltbush
Cistus spp.—Rockrose
Hypericum calycinum—Aaron's Beard
Teucrium chamaedrys—Germander

Drought Tolerant

Arctostaphylos spp.—Manzanita
Ariemesia caucasica—Caucasian Sagebrush
Atriplex spp.—Saltbush
Baccharis spp.—Coyote Bush
Ceanothus spp.—California Lilac
Cistus spp.—Rockrose

Hypericum calycinum—Aaron's Beard
Euonymus fortunei radicans—Wintercreeper
Lantana montevidensis—Trailing Lantana
Lonicera japonica 'Halliana'—Hall's Honeysuckle
Myoporum parvifolium prostrata
Rosmarinus officinalis 'Prostratus'—Creeping Rosemary
Salvia sonomensis—Creeping Sage
Santolina spp.—Lavender-cotton
Teucrium chamaedrys—Germander

OTHER PLANTS FOR FIRE BANDS

There are many other attractive landscape plants that may be combined with those of groups I, II, and III. These are primarily groundcovers and very small or low-growing perennials. They may have been omitted from the above groups for different reasons. Some simply haven't been tested. Others were not widely available nor adapted to extreme climates.

The key to selecting fire-band landscape plants is understanding the climate patterns of our Western states. Plants that flower and do most of their growing in winter, spring, and early summer can be cut back to minimal fuel volumes with the onset of fire season. For example, cool season annual flowers such as sweet peas or Iceland poppies go to seed with the heat, preferring the moderate temperatures of spring. They die back and are usually removed by the time fire season begins.

One of the groups most obviously well adapted to this regimen are hardy bulbs, which ensure a stunning spring garden but die back and almost disappear by fire season. Many are lifted and stored until replanting time in the fall while others are left in-ground year round. Among these are hyacinth, grape hyacinth, the daffodil clan, crocus, tulips, and Dutch iris. This group does not include tender summer bulbs such as gladiolas and dahlias.

In order to increase the choice of plants for firescapes, consider these plants for accent color or as substitutes when other plants listed here aren't available. They will require the same attention to detail in maintenance in order to keep fuel to a minimum and plants fully hydrated by regular irrigation. Do not plant them in masses, for this provides long avenues of unbroken fuels. Spot them in as singles, or in small, widely spaced groups.

Narcissus: Hardy spring bulbs begin flowering early in the season and are long gone by fire season. They are ideal plants for northern or high elevation land-scapes, with dozens of different types of narcissus, daffodils, and jonquils providing a diversity of spring color.

Annuals should be removed entirely after they go to seed or when their stems become overly dry.

The list below is some of the many common garden annuals and perennials that will add seasonal color to firescapes, especially in the band closest to the house where flowers are most appreciated. All have low growth, minimal fuel volume, and endurance into fire season if well cared for.

SELECTED NATIVE FLOWERS FOR FIRESCAPE BANDS

The chief qualities of all fire-resistant plants include high moisture content and low fuel volumes. For dry gardens where plant selection is limited by frost or lack of irrigation water, the regimen of the above lists may be broken with some bright color of native wildflowers. But consider only those species which are very low growing and tolerant of being cut back on a regular basis. Keep in mind that not all species of lupine, for example, are low growing, but there are short annual varieties that grow like a soft blue carpel in the infertile dry gravel of roadsides. California poppy is naturally low growing and perfect for spotting in color. Large quantities of seed for ground-hugging wildflowers can be obtained through the wildflower seed sources in the back of the book.

The following list includes some of the most reliable, but low-growing, wildflower species. Many seed suppliers have combined low-growing annuals and perennials into special seed mixtures ideal for firescaping. The annuals may be allowed to go to seed before mowing to produce next year's flower crop. Perennials naturally small in stature may remain year around to bloom each spring and summer. If you

California poppy should be sown in autumn to allow for its extensive roots to form while the rains fall. Only then will you have a spring bloom like this in your defensible space.

aren't an avid gardener and find these plant names mind boggling, it's best to stick with a specialized low-growing mix designed for your climate zone.

Botanical Name	Common Name	Height	Type
Anagallis arvensis	Pimpernel	10"	annual
Arabis alpina	Rockcress	8"	perennial
Campanula rotundifolia	Scotch Harebell	12"	perennial
Castilleja spp.	Indian Paintbrush	12"	annual
Centaurea cyanus	Dwarf Cornflower	12"	annual
Clarkia amoena	Dwarf Farewell-to-Spring	8"	annual
Coreopsis tinctoria nano	Dwarf Plains Coreopsis	18"	annual
Dianthus deltoides	Maiden Pinks	12"	perennial
Eschscholzia californica	California Poppy	14"	annual
Iberis umbellata	Candytuft	16"	annual
Iris missouriensis	Wild Blue Iris	12"	perennial
Layia platyglossa	Tidy-Tips	12"	annual
Leontopodium alpinum	Edelweiss	12"	perennial
Lupinus texensis	Texas Bluebonnet	12"	annual
Lychnis chalcedonica	Maltese Cross	12"	perennial
Nemophila maculata	Five-Spot	6"	annual
Nemophila menziesii	Baby Blue-Eyes	12"	annual
Oenothera missouriensis	Dwarf Primrose Evening	12"	perennial
Phacelia campanularia	California Bluebell	15"	annual
Silene armeria dwarf	Dwarf Catchfly	8"	annual

Many of the smaller shrubby wildflowers are more long lived, such as California fuchsia, monkey flowers, and the many penstemons native to western states. They all add interest to firescape bands, and if kept neatly pruned present very low fuel volumes. The tubular lipstick red flowers of California fuchsia attract hummingbirds. The soft apricot blossoms of monkey flower are a bit more finicky as they grow upon very steep rocky cliffs in foothill regions. Keep in mind that many western perennial wildflowers do much of their growing in late winter and spring, then slow down for dormancy during the heat and drought of late summer. This allows them to be cut back in time for fire season. These too should be purchased as plants in one-gallon containers because they do not readily grow from seed.

Mimulus sp.—Monkeyflower
Oenothera berlandieri—Mexican Evening Primrose
Zauschneria—California Fuchsia

Group IV Plant list

Plants with Low Growth Habits but Not Fire Resistant

Some of these plants are true groundcovers while others make colorful accents for interest and diversity in fire bands. Rarely grow taller than 12–18" and all are perennial.

Botanical Name	Common Name	Exposure	Flowers	Growth Habit	Comments
Agapanthus africanus 'Peter Pan'	Dwarf Lily of the Nile	Sun/Pt. shade	Blue	Tufts	Spacing: 18" Strap-leafed Zone 9
Alyssum saxatile	Basket of Gold	Sun/Pt. shade	Yellow	Spreading	Spacing: 24" Zone 3
Anthemis nobilis	Camomile	Sun	White	Spreading	Spacing: 6"–12" Mowable Zone 3
Armeria maritima	Thrift, Sea Pink	Sun/Pt. shade	Pink	Small tufts	Spacing: 12" Zone 3
Campanula poschar-skyana	Serbian Bell-flower	Pt. Shade	Blue	Spreading	Spacing: 6"–12" Mowable Zone 3
Coprosma prostrata	—	Pt. Shade	—	Spreading	Spacing: 24" Zone 9
Gazania splendens	Clumping Gazania	Sun	Many	Small mounds	Spacing: 12" Short lived Zone 9
Herniaria glabra	Green Carpet	Sun	—	Mat	Spacing: 6" Succulent Zone 9
Isotoma fluviatilis	Blue Star Creeper	Sun	Blue	Mat	Spacing: 6"–12" Hardy to 25 F
Liriope	'Silvery Sun-proof'	Pt. Shade	Purple	Small tufts	Spacing: 12" Strap-leafed Zone 6
Ophiopogon japonicum	Mondo Grass	Pt. Shade	—	Small tufts	Spacing: 6"–8" Strap-leafed Zone 6

OTHER LOW PROFILE COLOR PLANTS FOR FIRESCAPES

Perennials

Bellis perennis—English Daisy
Dianthus—China Pinks
Coreopsis auriculata nano—Dwarf Coreopsis
Heuchera sanguinea—Coral Bells
Iberis sempervirens—Candytuft
Impatiens hybrids—Impatiens
Phlox drummondii—Creeping Phlox
Vinca rosea—Dwarf Periwinkle

Annuals

Ageratum—Floss Flower
Lobularia maritima—Sweet Alyssum
Begonia semperflorens—Wax Begonia
Antirrhinum—Dwarf Snapdragons
Lobelia erinus—Annual Lobelia
Viola—Pansy, Viola
Primula hybrids—Primrose
Tagetes hybrids—Dwarf French Marigold

TREES IN FIRE BANDS

Just because there are no trees in the three fire-resistant plant groups doesn't mean there cannot be trees in a firescape. Trees provide shade, habitat, privacy, and improve the visual quality of a homesite. The key is knowing which ones to plant, where to put them within fire bands, and how to calculate proper spacings. Whenever possible keep them outside of zone 1, but if they must be dose to the house be sure you select a very small, slow-growing species. The further trees are away from the house the safer your site will be.

Not all trees are equally vulnerable to fire. It is well known that deciduous trees are more capable of resisting fire because they contain greater amounts of moisture, and when dormant and leafless there is far less fuel volume available. Ornamental varieties of deciduous or *broadleaf* evergreen trees closer to the house should be small in stature so fuel volumes are kept to a minimum. Of these, species with thick, succulent, and leathery leaves are the best choices, but they must be sufficiently irrigated to retain these qualities. Those which shed large amounts of leaves or peeling bark as well as other types of flammable litter are undesirable.

Conifers are evergreens that have needles instead of leaves. Typical examples are pine, juniper, and cypress. They contain oils and pitch that are extremely volatile. Accounts of early pine plantations of the Atlantic coastal plain describe how trees were tapped for their volatile pitch used to make turpentine. During drought there is less moisture content, and this situation mixed with the pitch makes a conifer even more flammable. Other trees such as the eucalyptus and acacia are loaded with similar oils, which contributed to the difficulties in the Berkeley Hills fire where these species were plentiful and very dry due to prolonged drought.

Trees also have another role in firescapes. Many with large root systems have been planted on hillsides to stabilize soil. If these trees are burned, their roots are still effective for erosion and will usually resprout from the stumps. Good choices for slopes are coast live oak (*Quercus agrifolia*), valley oak (*Quercus lobata*), alder (*Alnus rhombifolia* or *Alnus cordata*), and sycamore (*Platanus racemosus*).

FIRESCAPING TIP

Some species of shrubs and groundcovers also have the ability to resprout almost immediately after a fire, when encouraged by regular irrigation or rainfall. For very steep site with heavy dependence on vegetation to hold the slope, this ability is critical to soil stabilization. Incorporating these species into firescape slope planting ensures that there will be a network of living roots to hold the soil even though the aboveground portions have been burned off. Keep in mind that an extremely intense fire may ultimately kill the plants, but the lower fuel volumes in a firescape may keep temperatures down enough to help the plants survive. Look for the term "resprouts" in the fire-resistant plant lists to find ones with this unique quality.

There is information in the preceding chapter about thinning existing trees within fire bands. This applies primarily to native stands of varying species depending on the ecosystem, climate, and elevation. But if you have the choice of whether or not to plant trees, it's best to keep them widely spaced, and as far apart as you can manage. Burning trees produces flames sometimes twice as high as their crowns, which can send the fire towering over your rooftop.

You may be faced with the dilemma of shade versus fire safety. Shade trees reduce energy consumption (air conditioner), limit reflected heat from paving and bare ground, and make outdoor living possible in the hot summer months. Here lies the dilemma, which can only be resolved by taking into consideration site factors such as slope and exposure while evaluating the potential vulnerability to fires. With luck you will find a balance, which allows for a few carefully placed shade trees at the appropriate spacing.

In terms of native trees and as a model for shade trees, there should be a minimum of ten feet from the edge of the canopy of one tree to that of the next on level or gently sloping ground. For greater slopes this may be 20 or 30 feet depending on the exact percentages. This dimension is based upon the canopy limits of a mature tree, so when planning for ornamental trees choose and locate them according to their ultimate sizes.

Small Trees for Firescapes

(Frost tolerance varies, (E) = Evergreen)

Botanical Name	Common Name	Spring Flowers	Fall Color
Acer palmatum	Japanese Maple	—	yes
Cercis spp.	Redbud	yes	yes
Camus spp.	Dogwood	yes	yes
Crataegus spp.	Hawthorn	yes	berries
Lagerstroemia indica	Crape Myrtle	yes	—
Magnolia stellata	Star Magnolia	yes	—
Maytenus boaria (E)	Mayten Tree	—	—
Prunus subhirtella 'Pendula'	Weeping Japanese Cherry	yes	—

DECIDUOUS SHADE TREES FOR FIRESCAPES
(All acceptable as urban street trees)
Alnus cordata—Italian Alder
Ginkgo biloba—Maidenhair Tree
Liquidambar styraciflua—American Sweetgum
Liriodendron tulipifera—Tulip Tree
Pistacia chinensis—Chinese Pistache
Populus tremuloides—Quaking Aspen
Prunus cerasifera 'Atropurpurea'—Flowering Plum
Pyrus calleryana 'Bradford'—Bradford Pear
Quercus spp.—Oak

ARRANGING FIRE BAND PLANTS
One basic rule of all planting design is to use a variety of species rather than just one or two plant types. This ensures that if a disease or pests strike one variety of plant, the entire stand will not be destroyed. Another

Deciduous trees such as these sweetgums, *Liquidambar styraciflua*, provide beautiful fall color in warm climates, allow for wide spacing and maintain minimal fuel loads. Compare them to the immature ponderosa pine forest beyond; evergreen, volatile, filled with pitch.

concept is to prioritize plants, which becomes helpful if water rationing occurs in the future. A core group of durable and drought-tolerant spreading shrubs could make up the majority of the area, but interspersed could be expendable annual flowers or other colorful accents and groundcover plants. Under rationing, these core group would be spared at all costs while the rest could be allowed to die out.

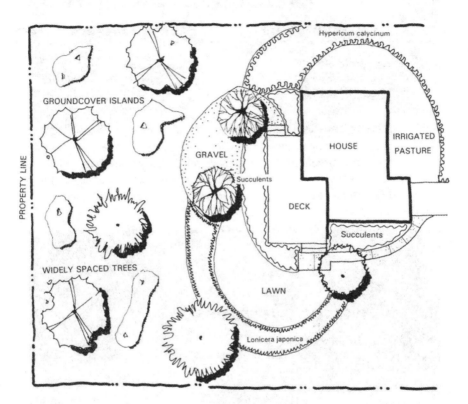

Sample Firescape Plan

This plan incorporates many of the plants and concepts of firescaping. Irrigated pasture and lawn provide plenty of green around the house while succulents are the only plants contacting the building walls. Outside are long bands of groundcovers and some widely spaced, small accent trees. The peripheral area is planted with drip-irrigated groundcover islands and shade trees. The remainder of the ground plain can be planted in annual grasses and/or wildflowers that die out at the end of spring and may be mowed short for minimal fuel availability and no watering requirements.

The house is protected by bands of planting that begin low and graduate upward as they ripple outward from the house to the barn. Utilizing many materials from gravel to paving and lawn are minimal fuels. Low heathers that love the coastal winds offer color over most of the year. There is plenty of access for firefighters and their equipment.

Here the builder used concrete and cobble to create a ribbon of stone around the base of the house walls and deck to physically separate ground fuels on fire from contact with the redwood siding. Beyond is a melange of low grasses and perennials, mowed just before fire season each year to separate the home from the redwood forest beyond.

Drought has increased the role of decorative gravel in landscaping, which also works well to separate plants or planted islands to slow or check fire movement due to the mineral mulch.

The French term *parterre* is used to describe gardens created with a series of planters in geometric shapes separated by gravel or paved walkways. This concept is ideal for fire-resistant landscapes because it separates areas of fuel. These formal planters are neatly bordered for water conservation and reduced maintenance. The planting scheme includes culinary herbs, annuals, perennials, and summer bulbs.

The heights and fuel volume of firescaping plants will vary according to how well they are pruned and maintained. Although all are low growing, try to create variety and take advantage of the growth habits by planting the taller varieties behind the shorter ones whenever you can. Intermix plants by arranging very small masses of each type rather than a hodgepodge of individuals. Let these drifts stand out from one another by contrasting flower color, foliage, and irregular textures. The more graceful your hand in selecting and locating your plants, the greater sense of unity the planting will display while still retaining sufficient diversity.

Planting areas can even be separated by narrow gravel walkways to increase their visual impact. This technique has been used for centuries in Europe where the walkways and planted areas are arranged in geometric patterns called a parterre. For ideas on formal firescape gardens study historic French formal landscapes and English knot gardens.

PASTURE LAND—THE MOST EFFECTIVE RURAL FIRESCAPE

Many rural homesites, farms, and ranches are blessed with high-producing wells or irrigation water supplies. In this case one of the most productive types of firescape techniques can be implemented: the irrigated pasture. This is simply an open space planted with a standard mixture of deep-rooted orchard grasses and clovers. Livestock turns this fire band into a productive agricultural crop for grazing and may even draw in hungry deer and elk during the dry season.

This same pasture technique can also be applied where there is no irrigated pasture. Cattle, horses, and sheep will graze a stand of annual grass down to nothing during the spring months leaving the area fuel-free in time for fire season. For this reason some carefully designed fencing will allow you to "import" livestock for awhile each year to do your grassland vegetation control without having to feed them the rest of the time. Should you want to clear out a brushland area the easy way, a herd of goats will be very effective on all types of shrubs including poison oak, though they aren't that fond of sagebrush. Pygmy goats are sometimes the best choice because bigger goats can climb over some types of fencing.

Livestock are an ideal way to manage large tracts of land to reduce ground level fuel loads on private property, and are being used on public lands with great success.

This illustrates how a larger homesite can be fire resistant by design. For example, a defensible home can be surrounded by irrigated pasture with just a few trees, and these may be kept clean of ladder fuels by nibbling horses or cows. Perhaps the driveway is routed around the house so

FIRESCAPING TIP

If you are not familiar with plants, it's worth the money to hire a professional landscape designer or landscape architect to prepare a planting plan for you. Using the concepts and plant lists in this book, the designer will be able to discuss what the final product will look like, and may even sketch it out in perspective. A skilled horticulturist is also helpful when blending native ecosystems with ornamental plants, which is a tricky venture when dealing with oaks and other sensitive plants that do not always tolerate root disturbance or unseasonable irrigation water.

Grassland mowed or grazed in spring dries out into a very short, blonde stubble for the summer which leaves very little for a fire to consume and requires no irrigation. The lower branches have been cleaned away from this redwood tree and there are no ladder fuels beneath the canopy.

it becomes a fire band free of any fuel at all. Corrals and ponds also offer excellent opportunities for home protection.

RISKY BUSINESS: VOLATILE LANDSCAPE PLANTS TO AVOID

This list contains some of the conifers included in the frost-hardy plant list. These plants are to be avoided in warmer climates, but where cold winters limit choices they are allowable, but only if properly arranged.

Acacia spp.	Acacia
Bougainvillea	Bougainvillea
Cedrus spp.	Cedar
Cortaderia selloana	Pampas Grass
Cupressus spp.	Cypress
Dodonaea spp.	Hopseed Bush
Eucalyptus spp.	Eucalyptus
Gelsemium sempervirens	Carolina Jessamine
Hakea suaveolens	Hakea
Juniperus spp.	Juniper
Pennisetum spp.	Fountain Grass
Pinus spp.	Pines
Phormium tenax	New Zealand Flax
All ornamental grasses	
All berry vines	

7

LONG-TERM MAINTENANCE OF PLANTS AND EQUIPMENT

This is the most important chapter in the book because proper care and upkeep of a firescape and firefighting systems is critical to whether or not they function when needed. For example, lack of long-term attention can result in fire-resistant plants loading up with dead twigs, leaves, and branches to grow into monstrous, yet sometimes invisible fuel volumes. Accumulations of needles and leaves upon a rooftop may transform Class B roofing material into a flammable hazard. Rodents in the pump house, earwigs dogging the sprinkler heads, and decaying hoses could seriously disable, if not eliminate, the benefit of your emergency water supply.

There are four main categories of a proper maintenance program:

1. Care of plants.
2. Fine tuning of irrigation systems.
3. Testing and protection of emergency water supply and delivery systems.
4. Attention to house and outbuildings.

Each of these categories is equally important because neglect of one may render the others ineffective. For example, if you allow the fireband plants to become overgrown and develop high fuel volumes, your emergency water system may not be capable of resisting the much taller and more intense flames resulting from the additional vegetation.

CATEGORY 1: CARE OF PLANTS

Plants in firescapes may be comprised of existing native species, ornamental plants or both. Obviously, plants are unlike a house or other buildings that remain the same over many decades: Every day your trees grow a bit larger, shrubs spread out, and the litter of fallen leaves thickens. This is the natural increase of the earth's biomass, which ultimately leads to rising fuel volumes in firescapes unless properly managed.

Whether your plants are native or ornamental, it's best to think about proper care in terms of fuels and fire types. As detailed in other chapters, fuels occur in three locations and may be either live or dead materials. Surface fires feed off fuels dose to the ground. Dead surface fuels include leaves and needles, fallen twigs, cones, and bark. Live surface fuels are comprised of living leaves and needles still attached to plants, low branches, weeds, and other plant material within the first few feet above the ground.

Aerial fuels are mainly living and dead parts of tree tops—the main components of crown fires. Tree canopies too close together provide a clear avenue of fuel. Ladder fuels occur in between ground and aerial fuels These include tall shrubs or drooping foliage, as well as lower branches that have died back, fallen snags, stumps, and anything else that will provide a "rung in the ladder" upon which a fire rises to tree tops, or drops from the trees down to ground level.

All these factors have been reviewed because they are the reasons why maintenance is essential to a fire-resistant landscape. It's easiest to divide tasks according to the fuel types so that you can make the proper decisions as to what must be done, and how frequently the job must be repeated. Because every homesite is different, the duties required will vary in kind. An effective maintenance program must always be tailored to meet the individual needs of the site.

MANAGEMENT OF GROUND FUELS

SPRING Remove any frost-damaged plants or prune back burned leaves and branches. Control plant heights. Rake up litter caused by winter storms. First mowing of natural grasses. Plant new seed or plants as required for replacement. Renew thinning mulches. Control weeds manually or with herbicide while actively growing. Fertilize.

SUMMER   Cut back spent flowers. Prune back wayward growth. Second or third natural grass mowing May–June. Control weeds. Irrigate well.

FALL   Control weeds. Irrigate well. Remove plants going to seed. Rake up fallen autumn leaves. Remove all weeds. Mow if necessary. Replant as needed. Fertilize (optional).

WINTER   Prune back summer growth. Burn slash with valid permit. Seed wildflowers and grasses before winter rain. Replant as needed.

AN OVERVIEW OF TASKS

There are some basic activities required for management of all firescape plants. Understanding the exact definition of these terms makes the maintenance guidelines in this chapter easier to understand.

Pruning   This is the methodical cutting back of plant parts to reduce the overall size, or to remove dead twigs or branches. Also includes thinning of tree canopies and reducing the tops of tall shrubs.

Litter Reduction   This activity gathers and removes any unwanted dead materials from the soil surface. It does not apply to decorative mulches.

Weed Control   Removal of existing weeds both alive or dead. Includes ground treatments of various types to discourage the growth of new weeds.

Revegetation   Replacement of any plants that have died out in order to reduce soil erosion or for aesthetic purposes.

Mowing   Open spaces treated with irrigated pasture, lawn, or when renewing "mowable" groundcovers. If possible, cut with a rotary lawn mower on a regular basis and dispose of the clippings. Naturally occurring annual grasses that die out in late spring also require mowing or trimming and chaff removed. large-scale sites may be cut with a tractor and flail mower.

Removal   Remnants of dead plants, fallen trees, branches, or stumps. Thinning out of living plants that have outgrown space allotted to them.

MANAGEMENT OF AERIAL FUELS

This applies to canopies of all trees, evergreen, and deciduous. Aerial fuels include both living branches and accumulations of litter such as dead needles still attached or resting on the limbs. Pruning is the main activity, with attention focused on decreasing canopy diameters that may encroach on the open space between each tree. Trees with excessive amounts of branches that create heavy fuel loads must also be thinned every few years. Canopy reduction, or thinning, is best done in winter and early spring while growth is slower and fire danger minimal. This is also the wet season, when chainsaws are less of a hazard, and where permitted the materials may be immediately burned. A chipper/shredder machine turns this refuse into valuable mulch. Removal of dead limbs in deciduous trees is best done during summer because they are only visible when tree is fully leafed out.

Management of aerial fuels includes canopy reduction, thinning, and removal of any dead limbs. A pole pruning device with a saw attached to the end allows you to reach branches high in the canopy without the danger of climbing trees.

LADDER FUELS

A well-designed firescape should not have any ladder fuels, but sometimes they gradually develop unnoticed over long periods of time. As trees grow taller, more of the low branches may be pruned away as long as they don't comprise more than one-third of the total height. Taller native shrubs in the outermost band may also gain some height, and if dose enough to a tree they could act as a ladder fuel. There must be clear space between the top of the shrub and the lowest tree branch. This space should be roughly three times the height of the shrub.

CATEGORY 2: FINE TUNING OF IRRIGATION SYSTEMS

There are two reasons why fine tuning of irrigation systems is so important. First, it is the only means of keeping a firescape alive and functional so there is sufficient moisture in the plants for them to resist fire. Second, water is a precious resource and should be used as efficiently as possible, not only because it reduces our water bills, but so the system is still able to function under drought conditions.

For those using standard irrigation systems, the lines will be underground with only the risers and/or heads visible. The problem that most frequently occurs with these systems is clogged or malfunctioning heads. Clogging can be caused by insects in the lines or particulate matter such as calcium that may break free from the pipes to block the nozzles. Gear-driven or pop-up heads may not operate if grains of soil or other matter become jammed in the mechanism. If heads are bumped they can be forced out of adjustment, delivering water where it is not needed and leaving the intended area partially dry. To ensure all the heads are operating properly and there are no underground leaks or cracks, test the system at least four times per year to check coverage and output.

Drip systems are a bit more difficult to check because they have a network of tubing and emitters hidden under plants and mulch. There are dozens of ways tubing can become damaged, so it should be checked for leaks at least four times a year, but preferably more often. Emitters can also clog up, and if these are not checked monthly you may never know it is blocked until the plant wilts or dies. To reduce clogging, use insect

THE PINE BARK BEETLE

Various species of bark beetles have attacked stands of pine timber throughout our forests. The beetles have always been here, but when trees are stressed by drought the pests are better able to reproduce. They will attack the weakest individuals first, and there are plenty of these since our forests are overcrowded due to the lack of cleansing landscape fires. The beetles are one of nature's culling mechanisms to weed out weaker trees and keep forests healthy.

These insects invade trees through the soft growing tip at the very top or tips of side branches. This is why trees typically die from the top down, or from side branch tips inward. Normally there is sufficient water pressure within the trees to exclude the beetles, but prolonged drought reduces it enough to allow the beetles to enter and lay their eggs. These hatch out into voracious larvae that burrow through the cambium layer beneath the bark, destroying the tree's ability to transport moisture and nutrients. Eventually the larvae mature and pupate into flying adults, which then leave the host tree to lay yet more eggs at the top of the next suitable individual. It is recommended that any trees or tree parts that contain beetle eggs or larvae be burned immediately and not transported elsewhere to further extend the beetle's territory.

resistant emitters and install a filter on each valve of the system to strain out sediment in the water supply. Clean out the filter frequently or it will become full and reduce flow rates.

Microspray tubing is equally as vulnerable but it's easier to check for clogged emitters because the spray heads are visible. These systems also benefit from filters and should be checked frequently. As plants grow larger it is necessary to reposition the heads to ensure adequate coverage. The gradual moisture reduction in your firescape plants from malfunctioning irrigation systems may not be visible until it is too late to quickly rehydrate them again.

CATEGORY 3: EMERGENCY WATER SUPPLY AND DELIVERY SYSTEMS

Wildfires can start and threaten your homesite in an instant, leaving absolutely no time to fuss with equipment. Discovering your supply line is riddled with holes when a fire is at your doorstep is a deadly serious matter. Ask any professional firefighter and you may be surprised at how often their hoses are inspected and replaced, just to be sure.

The emergency water reservoir should be well marked so that firefighters may utilize it when protecting your home. It must be kept full at all times and checked frequently, especially in hot weather. Keeping the water free of debris that might clog the suction hose of a pump is also important. Even if you have a screen on the end of the hose, it can become encased in leaves and the suction will hold the blockage against the screen as long as you are pumping. Clouds or strings of algae can also clog the small screen holes, but an occasional dose of swimming pool chlorine will help reduce this problem.

Hoses can become a real menace if not properly cared for. They should be reserved exclusively for fire-flow systems and not used in the garden. Keep them in the same location at all times, a place protected from rodents, insects, and both direct sun and winter cold. Coil loosely on a flat, dry surface so there is less tendency for kinking or corkscrew stiffness when in use. Store the nozzles with hoses.

Any roof watering apparatus constructed out of white PVC pipe should be stored away from direct sunlight. This material is designed to be either buried or used indoors. It will break down if subjected to direct sunlight and extremes of temperature over time. There are no visible signs of weakened PVC except perhaps a slight discoloration, but it will become overly brittle and crack under very little pressure.

People in cold winter states know too well the damage that can occur when water freezes inside pipes, automobile engines, and, most important, water pumps. Whether driven by an electric motor or a gasoline engine, small amounts of water remain inside the pump, and if it is allowed to freeze there can be major equipment damage. If you have operated your pump at all, it is essential you remove *all* the freeze plugs before exposing the pump to freezing temperatures. This also applies to hoses and any other apparatus which may contain sufficient amounts of water stored outdoors or in uninsulated buildings.

CATEGORY 4: HOUSE AND OUTBUILDINGS

This applies not only to your house but to any sheds, barns, stables, garages, or structures of any kind of your property. Even the most fireproof roofing will become volatile if covered with a layer of pine needles or leaves. Keep the roof as clean as possible all year round, and remove debris from rain gutters. The new fascia gutters are deeper than the older styles and a

SMALL ENGINE MAINTENANCE

Most generators and engine-driven water pumps rely on a four-cycle engine. Anyone who has struggled with a reluctant lawnmower knows how temperamental they can be after sitting for awhile. It is essential this equipment is stored properly and operated at regular intervals to ensure it functions when needed.

It's a good idea to purchase a book on small gasoline engines for basics on storage and maintenance. One of the primary issues is the fuel itself. New gasoline blends tend to contain methanol and other additives that are not good for small engines. Try to buy only name-brand high octane supreme gas. Gasoline also tends to separate and evaporate, leaving sludge if left to sit for any period of time. When the small engine is stored with gas still in the fuel tank, fuel lines, and carburetor, the sludge is likely to foul the engine or make it hard to start later on.

To be on the safe side, run your generator or pump out of gas after each test or use. Store gas in a separate container and replace the supply every month or two, particularly during fire season. If the engine is needed in an emergency, have a funnel handy so you can fill or refill the tank quickly and fire it up. For electric starting engines, consult the manufacturer regarding storage and specific requirements of the battery. Change the oil in the engine at least once a year.

greater quantity of leaves can build up before they become visible at the top. Because rain gutters are rarely in use during fire season, they are often full and hazardous. Although they are not part of the structure, remove all flammable plants or weeds along building foundations.

OTHER FIREFIGHTING EQUIPMENT

Whether it is you or firefighters who protect your house, a number of essential tools must be kept at hand. These should be separate from hand tools used for gardening or cleaning. Keep them stored where they will be available at a moment's notice. They include one or more of the following: a large metal bucket, rake, shovel, pruning saw, axe, and lopping shears. A gasoline-operated chainsaw can be helpful as well. Have two or more watertight plastic garbage cans available to fill with water and station at important points around the house if fire threatens. You'll also need a ladder to gain access to your roof, and for larger houses two ladders might be more useful so there is one at either end.

8

WHAT TO DO WHEN
THE FIRE COMES

Many state forestry agencies have developed instructive videos which show you the conditions that spark wildfire disasters. In any emergency situation, there will be those who panic and thus fail to make logical decisions during the critical moments when fire approaches. Above all, it is essential to stay calm and attend to the activities necessary to ensure the safety of your family and hopefully that of your home as well. The key is to have a well-detailed fire plan established *ahead of time* so that each person knows exactly what to do.

PUT TOGETHER A SURVIVAL PACK

Expectant mothers have traditionally packed up important items in an overnight bag well before the delivery date. The bag is ready to go at a moment's notice. Preparing for a fire is done much the same way because if you must evacuate suddenly, which often occurs during wildfires, everything will be ready to make this difficult situation less frantic. In fact, it's also a good idea in case of a house fire as well. There are two groups of items that should be considered. First, there are the basic necessities—a change of clothes, medicines, toiletries, a coat, list of important phone numbers, and other essential everyday items. For those living in remote or rural areas, additional items are even more essential because goods and services will not be close by.

A SURVIVAL EVACUATION PACK

1. **Leather hiking boots with heavy soles** Synthetic materials may melt in hot ash.
2. **Flashlight with fresh batteries** Replace batteries annually or include second set.
3. **Canteen** Keep it full of water if you live far from any rivers, lakes, or other water sources. Use a large one to be sure there is sufficient water to wet your clothing as well as for drinking.
4. **Large cotton bandanna** It can be soaked in water and tied around your nose and mouth to filter smoke. Synthetic fibers are less absorbent and may melt.
5. **Heavy, long-sleeved shirt** Thickly woven wool or cotton, which may be soaked to better insulate against heat and resist embers.
6. **High-energy snack foods** These are found in all survival packages and will keep indefinitely in original containers. Chocolate, granola bars, trail mix, etc.
7. **Lightweight, compact, first aid kit** Add extra salve for burns. Include a supply of important prescription medications.
8. **Rescue location aids** A metal whistle and neck lanyard for ground searchers. A 6 x 6 foot square of florescent orange nylon helps to locate you from the air.
9. **Construction hard hat** Protects your hair from hot embers that fill the skies in all wildfires. Protects against head injuries in forests where there is the risk of falling branches or even entire trees.
10. **A sturdy backpack** If you must travel for a long distance, having all these items in a comfortable backpack is a lifesaver, particularly when both hands must be free to climb steep terrain.

HOMESITE SURVIVAL TIPS

If there is a fire in your area, utility lines and telephone poles are often burned. Although your house may not be threatened, if the lines supporting your services are cut, you may be without power for some time. Survival during and after a fire may also mean you must be able to function without water or electrical supplies. This is also helpful in case of

WILDFIRE TIP

Whenever there is a natural disaster, telephone communication may be cut off and your radio may be the only means of keeping in touch with the size of a wildfire and in which direction it is likely to move. The best way to be well informed both at home or after evacuation is through a handheld radio scanner with both police and radio frequencies. You will know exactly what firefighting agencies and police are doing at all times. Be sure to keep fresh batteries with the scanner and a spare set for backup. You can also listen to it during fire weather to keep up on smaller brush fires that inevitably pop up at this time of year. Most retail electronics stores offer reasonably priced models.

earthquake, tornado, or other natural disasters. Forest fire agencies suggest each house be equipped with the following:

1. Three-day supply of food sufficient for the entire family; foods that do not require refrigeration nor cooking and will store indefinitely.
2. Three-day supply of drinking water can be stored in sealed gallon milk jugs, water cooler, or plastic liter bottles.
3. Assortment of survival aids such as a portable radio, flashlight, extra batteries, emergency cooking equipment, fuel, and portable lantern.
4. First aid kit and medical supplies.

PREPARING TO EVACUATE

Fires never occur when expected and often families are fragmented, with adults in one place and one or more of the children somewhere else. It is important that everyone understands there is a second location where all are to meet up eventually. This may be the home of a relative or close friend within a few miles from home.

The sudden order to evacuate leaves many homeowners in a quandary as to which of their cherished possessions to load into the car. Consider keeping some of them permanently in a safe deposit box or fireproof safe to reduce the number of things to take away during evacuation. The confusion around fires can be terrifying, so a list prepared ahead of time for quick consultation assists in gathering up these essential items with the least amount of stress.

1. **Legal documents** These include birth certificates, deeds, stock certificates, and other essential paperwork. Discuss with your accountant and/or attorney about which ones are most important. This also applies to your fire insurance papers, too, because you will need them if your home or property is damaged.

2. **Photographs** These cannot be replaced at any cost and are often the most sadly mourned when lost in a house fire. Store negatives at a separate location.

3. **Mementos** Heirlooms, art work, and other keepsakes.

4. **Jewelry and other valuables** Gold, precious stones, coins, fine art, family silver, antiques, etc.

5. **Family pets**

6. **Computer Files** If you have an office at home or store vital records and data in your computer, be sure to keep all your files backed up off site or in the cloud. A small external hard drive allows you to grab and run with large archives.

ARRANGEMENTS FOR ANIMALS

The recent fires which threatened the Santa Inez Valley, a community of horse ranches that also included valuable cattle and other farm animals. Many of the residents did not have an evacuation plan for their horses, nor did some have access to horse trailers. Most horse trailers will hold only two animals, and where more were present at the homesite, numerous trips were required to ferry them to safety. Often there is not enough time for such luxury.

This illustrates the complications of evacuating animals, particularly when you should be free to defend your house. Animals have survival instincts that cause them to panic at the smell of smoke. Cats and dogs will either run and/or hide and may never be found by the time evacuation is ordered. It is best to purchase secure pet carrying crates for each small animal, and be sure to have them loaded into the car or off site well ahead of time. A recent sad example of what could happen was the Southern California man who went back to his house after the evacuation order to rescue a house cat. The man never returned and was consumed by the flames. No animal is worth your life or that of any member of your family.

We have all heard tales of large animals such as horses led from a burning barn to safety, then turn and run back "home" into the burning barn. This is a reality, and simply opening the gates to allow the livestock to fend for themselves is not the answer. Trailering large animals, especially when they are excited and afraid, is no simple matter and can be very dangerous. What most people don't consider is where to take the animals, and even more important, who will take care of them once they get there. It is likely you will have to return to the house for other animals or to fight the fire, and without prior arrangements for someone to stable your horses or cattle, you may face a serious dilemma.

If you own livestock, prepare an evacuation plan ahead of time. Even if premature, getting animals out of the area is essential, not only for their safety, but to free you for more important duties. If you don't have a trailer, this allows time to obtain one. Neighbors can be surprisingly generous with their trailers under these conditions, but only after their animals are taken care of. Know exactly where you are going and how long it takes to get there, so if there must be a number of trips you'll allow enough time.

IN THE LINE OF FIRE—EVACUATION IS IMMINENT

As the fire approaches you may be waiting for the evacuation order. It is wise to evacuate the children and those disabled, ill, or very old before the official order if it looks like the fire is coming toward you. If you are not prepared to defend the house, or lack emergency water supplies, make last minute preparations to the house and then leave as soon as evacuation is ordered.

If you have a swimming pool, you can save your china, silver, glassware and other items that aren't damaged by water. If the house burns these items will be ruined as it collapses. To save them simply load the items in plastic garbage bags, poke lots of holes in the bag so it won't float, tie off the top and drop it carefully into the deep end of the pool. There at the bottom they will be protected and insulated by the water until you retrieve them later on.

There are many things you can do to make the house itself better able to resist ignition and assist firefighters when they arrive. First, you must dress for fire because on the front lines there is a perpetual rain of embers or firebrands. They are most apparent when seen at night glowing bright orange in the dark sky, but only black specks during the day. Some can be very large and cause sizeable burns if they land on your skin. The emphasis on cotton and not synthetic fabrics in the survival packs is because synthetic fibers melt before they burn, and will stick to your skin. No matter how hot the weather, fire experts recommend you dress in long pants and a wool or cotton long-sleeve shirt. The more layers you wear, the less chance of an ember burning through to your skin. Gloves, a dampened bandanna, and nonsynthetic hat are also important.

Load up your getaway car with everything you plan to take with you. Park it in the garage facing out, roll up the windows tightly, and put the keys in the ignition. Close the garage door completely and disconnect the automatic opener so that if the power goes out you can still open the door. Think ahead and plan an evacuation route which will lead away from the fire's path. To stay abreast of the fire behavior, keep a portable radio and/or scanner with you at all times. A flashlight is also valuable when the smoke gets thick, or if you are still there at night fall. To prepare your house for resisting the fire and assist firefighters when they arrive, first board up all the vents and windows. The firefighters must drag hoses and move around quickly, so pull any obstacles such as lawn furniture, grills, planters, toys, bicycles, as well as flammable items away from the building.

If you have an emergency water system, make sure it is set up and tested, and a clear path exists so fire trucks can access your reservoir. Where no system is in place, hook up garden hoses to every spigot around the house so they are ready. Set up a sprinkler on your roof, but if you are on a municipal water system don't turn it on until absolutely necessary as this may reduce water pressure for firefighters somewhere else. Fill all your trash cans and buckets up to the top with water and be sure firefighters know they are there. Place one or more ladders against the house to assist in accessing the roof.

Once the outside is secure and ready, go indoors and be sure each windows and door is completely closed—but not locked. Turn on all the

COVERINGS FOR WALL OPENINGS

Frequently overlooked, air vents into attics and crawl spaces become avenues for embers to contact flammable materials indoors. These openings should be covered up with half an inch or thicker plywood when embers start to fly so they are completely blocked off. You can also cover the outsides of windows with plywood to help insulate them from the heat. Have these panels precut and stored along with a hammer and double-headed foundation nails so they are ready for use. When the fire gets close is not the time lo rush around scrounging for material and a saw.

lights. Fill every sink, bathtub, and other large containers with water. Shut off any or all natural gas or liquid propane gas (LPG) valves—you should know of where each one is well ahead of time. Move flammable window coverings and other household furnishings away from windows. These can be ignited from intense heat radiating through unprotected windows and glass doors. Once all these tasks have been completed, you can leave or remain behind if there is sufficient water and equipment to douse any ember-generated spot fires around the house.

When the fire is at your door, the heat around the house will be intense. **Don't wait until this point to evacuate because it is already too late.** It is safest to remain inside but do not lock the doors. Keep everyone together and resist going outside. This is a very dangerous emergency situation and ideally everyone should have evacuated by this time. Homeowners with protective firescaping may not experience such intense heat close to the house and are more likely to survive, but firestorm conditions more recently have become far more intense and are occurring at night. In fact, fire behavior is becoming less and less predictable with such enormous fuel accumulations and high winds. If an emergency fire system is operational, remember you have a finite amount of water. Turning it on too soon may cause a shortage later when the fire is much closer. The exact timing is up to you, but it should be operating and make the surrounding surfaces wet before the flames reach the house.

After the Malibu fires in 1993, a couple was found in their charred pickup truck, clearly trying to evacuate, but time ran out. They were attempting to drive down a narrow, vegetation choked dirt road at the last minute. It's not difficult to imagine what the scene must have been like, which proves how important cleared access is to the defensible home-site. The couple must have encountered walls of flame on both sides of the road—a tunnel of fire. This is why it is recommended you keep the roadway edges cleared of fuel so that access and evacuation are occur unhindered.

This can happen to anyone who insists on remaining behind beyond the point of reason. If you are trapped, try to drive to an open area where fuel volumes are lowest. Stop, close vehicle windows and vents, cover yourself with a blanket or coat, and lie on the floor. When evacuating on foot, find a similarly open area and avoid canyons. If you can locate a ditch or swale, lie down flat in the bottom and cover yourself as you would in the car. Ideally a lake, pond, or other open water body not crowded with vegetation is the safest point.

AFTER THE FLAMES PASS

After the fire has roared through your homesite the danger is not over. If you were fortunate, the house will be still standing, but embers may be lodged in nooks and crannies of roofs, siding, and wood decks. Inspect the entire structure closely and douse any hot spots that remain. Climb up into the attic and check for embers there as well. Do not open the windows right away because the fire is still burning and if the wind shifts it may send ash back in your direction. Walk the property and search for smoking hot spots or burning woodpiles, trees, plants, fences, firewood, outbuildings, and other combustible materials. Look for signs of ground fires that may simply be smoldering in the soil because these can flare up days later. Pay dose attention to any native trees or shrubs in the outer fire bands. Continue these inspections frequently over the next twelve hours, and keep an eye on any signs of smoke for at least a week.

9

AFTER THE FIRE: EROSION CONTROL AND REVEGETATION

The majority of the West's most damaging wildfires occur during the fire season, which extends from early summer to late fall. The rains can be so unpredictable that the duration of dry fall weather varies considerably from year to year. But in all cases the fire season is ended by the onset of winter rains, and here lies the second great danger.

Many of the most fire-prone ecosystems occur in foothill and mountain areas. Once these slopes are denuded of vegetation they become highly susceptible to soil erosion, which is proven after nearly every fire by reports of large scale mud slides. Although the fire may not have touched your homesite, it may still be vulnerable to the effects of erosion in other areas within the same watershed. If the land did burn, and whether or not the house was saved, the threat of destabilization of slopes is very real.

Post-fire aerial views of steep hillside subdivisions with every home burned to the ground reveals how tentative the actual foundation area can be. Those homes perched on tiny cut-and-fill pads or split-level footings are vulnerable to total slope failure. These unfortunate residents stand to lose not only the building, but also the actual pads and slopes themselves, which can simply disintegrate under saturation from winter rain. The other aspect to this scenario is that those homes still standing below these burned-out sites are in the path of the mud slides. Add a mild earthquake and the problem increases.

There are various forms of erosion that relate to how they are controlled, either by short-term emergency methods, and/or long-term

After a fire sweeps through foothill and mountain areas, steep slopes such as this one are vulnerable to rain, mudslides, and even avalanches during the winter. Whether or not the slopes support plant life the first year depends on the depth of soil damage.

Single homes that survive a fire when all around them has burned to the ground are miraculous. This one, like many built in ski resort communities, rests on a tiny bench for the building pad. With so little surface area, serious erosion can cause the pads of burned houses to simply vanish altogether in a mudslide. With such great erosion potential all around it, this survivor faces a second threat of slope destabilization as sites above and below fight the potential failure.

When the vegetation on giant slopes such as this one burns off, the soil is at great risk, and with nothing to slow the speed of runoff, there will be a potential for land at the bottom to be flooded with runoff. Diversion ditches have been dug to traverse the surface and carry water away from the critical points, but on this scale it seems hardly adequate.

Under the guidance of federal, state, and county agencies, crews of workers must be at a fire site to shore up burned slopes such as these which become serious hazards after losing their protective covering of vegetation. In this case, both highway dividers as well as hundreds of sand bags will help, but not completely resolve, the erosion problem.

IMPORTANT DEFINITIONS

Erosion   The detachment and transportation of soil particles by the forces of water (cause).

Sedimentation   The deposit of suspended particles of soil in areas where water movement slows down (effect).

stabilization techniques, or both. Erosion always results in sediment deposits somewhere else, which is too often a stream bed, river, pond, or lake. The more sediment deposited in these waterways, the more limited their capacity. Therefore erosion control is also an effort to keep waterways healthy and preserved.

Erosion can be caused by any kind of soil disturbance, such as grading, cultivation, logging, or by fires, which may expose vast areas of once-forested ground, rendering them vulnerable to soil erosion. In recent fires the soil becomes hydrophobic and repels water, a condition which prevents seeds from sprouting to hold the surface.

Soil erosion is not just confined to steep slopes; it can occur on nearly level ground if there is sufficient water movement. If these sites are burned, they too will require some erosion control measures to reduce topsoil losses and prevent siltation into local drainages. The need for an immediate erosion control plan is greater on newly burned steep sites due to the increased potential for large-scale mudslides.

FACTORS IN CHOOSING EROSION CONTROL METHODS

Every drop of rain that falls on bare soil will dislodge a few soil particles, even on an absolutely level site. The degree of slope upon which the particle rests determines whether or not it moves away, and the speed at which it is carried by flowing water. Take a mild slope and add a few hundred thousand raindrops and you have quite a bit of moving soil. This illustrates how erosion control methods must first protect the soil surface from the impact of the raindrop so that the particles remain in place. Second, the controls must slow the movement of water down the slope so that the particles drop out sooner and are not carried further down.

If you were to study a rock or tree branch on bare ground after a heavy rain you would notice that on the uphill side there is usually a deposit of fine sand or silt. The rock or branch became an obstacle in the movement of the water, forcing its velocity to slow for a time, and when water slows down the suspended soil particles drop out. Think back to this example when reviewing the erosion-control suggestions in order to better understand how they function on your site.

Finally, the goal of revegetation is to prolong the protection of soil surface particles and bind them into a stronger mass. Plants are the best and least expensive erosion control method we have, but they take time to mature and become most effective. Revegetating with fire-resistant plants will help protect your home from fire if it occurs again.

THE EFFECTS OF FIRE ON SOIL

Wildfires vary in their intensity and duration. Grass fires burn for a short time and at relatively low temperatures. They can actually increase soil fertility. Fires in dense brush and overgrown forests burn much hotter due to the greater proportion of heavy wood fuels such as trees and shrubs. The temperature as well as length of time the fire burns will influence a number of different soil characteristics.

Soils are made up of mineral nutrients, organic matter and microorganisms all bound together by complex chemical reactions. When superheated by intense wildfires, and continuing for a short while after the fire, organic matter is burned away, nitrogen is consumed, and microorganisms are killed. Many types of grass seed in the upper levels of the soil may also die. The result is considerable decrease in soil fertility, and reduced ability of the area to regenerate quickly from existing seed and thus naturally check surface erosion.

After fires, it is typically the legumes (certain members of the pea family) that are first able to sprout and grow. That's because they obtain nitrogen from the atmosphere, and with special microorganisms in their root systems actually transfer it to the soil. They need not rely on soil nitrogen to survive. Other plants are prevented from thriving as do the legumes because they are starved for nutrients destroyed by the heat.

From this we know soils subjected to intense fires must be enriched with organic matter in the form of humus. Typical sources are manure or compost. The soil also benefits from applications of synthetic chemical fertilizers as well to help emergency erosion control grasses get off to a quick start. Since these sites are often on hillsides, fertilizers applied in liquid form help the nutrients to soak directly into the soil and become immediately available. Dry granules require copious amounts of water to dissolve and enter the soil, but the expectant rains will do this job. On gentle slopes and nearly flat land revegetated by seed, granules become a more convenient means of increasing soil nutrient content. For large-scale reforestation, the US Forest Service uses aerial applications of granular fertilizers.

Another effect of high heat exposure is a change in soil structure. The heat not only causes deeper soil moisture to evaporate, it also cements soil particles of certain types into very dense layers. Think of this as the difference between ceramic clay and the fired, finished product that is far more cohesive and durable. The hotter the fire (as with a kiln) the more impenetrable the soil becomes. Experts say soil exposure to temperatures of 482° F for at least ten minutes is the minimum required to initiate the cementation effect.

These fired soils are technically hydrophobic because the earth becomes reluctant or refuses to absorb moisture. In the past, the average depth of this condition following fires was at the most four inches deep, but in the last five years, the immense violent wildfires have produced layers nearly fourteen inches deep over very large areas. This causes a serious increase in runoff during the rains or spring thaw. This faster moving water is also more likely to dislodge surface particles outside burn areas and cause unwanted erosion and siltation. Moreover, this concrete-like surface presents an inhospitable seedbed for germination of erosion-control plants or return of native vegetation.

We know the binding effect on soil structure is temporary and will break down, usually within a year. To speed this process the soil may be rototilled or ripped by heavy equipment if not on slopes. Surface scarification with rakes or other hand implements helps seeds to lodge and germinate without risking serious erosion. Mulching of seeds after broadcasting also helps to hold them in place, checking surface flow and siltation.

Erosion controls for burn sites are divided into emergency methods and long-term stabilization techniques. In warmer climates with heavy winter rains such as the Pacific Coast portions of Washington and Oregon, there is a propensity for mudslides in hillside subdivisions. There immediate emergency methods are critical during the first weeks and months following a fire to protect the surface of the soil as well as reduce siltation. A more long-term erosion control plan is based on a permanent firescape band system of landscaping as well as drainage structures, cobblestone riprap, and diversion ditches.

EMERGENCY EROSION CONTROL MEASURES

These techniques can be divided into two categories: those using man-made materials, and those relying on plants. The best choice depends on the degree of slope, soil type, availability of irrigation, cost, and risk of large-scale slope failure. Another factor is the ability to channel runoff away from the slope and thereby reduce the erosion control potential.

PLASTIC SHEETING Where landslide threat is imminent or when soils on steep slopes are overly saturated, this temporary method separates rain drops from the soil entirely. The plastic must be anchored above the top of the slope so runoff cannot travel underneath the sheet. Attach the top edge per anchor trench diagram. Use only heavy-gauge plastic and stake or bury all edges to avoid tearing by wind. A disadvantage is that as long as the plastic remains in place it prevents erosion control plants from growing, and will soon weaken from exposure to sunlight.

STRAW MULCH This is the most widely used immediate erosion control method because it is totally organic, inexpensive, widely available, and easy to transport in neat bale form. A straw mulch not only protects the soil from surface erosion but acts as a filter for sediment. If the slope is to be seeded, broadcast the seed before you apply the straw mulch. Distribute the straw in an even layer at least 3 inches thick but loose enough to still see the soil beneath. Estimate approximately 2 tons per acre.

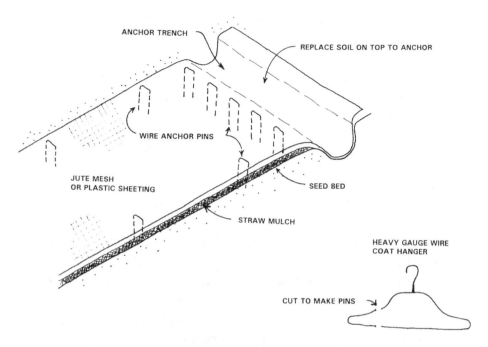

Anchor and Application Diagram for Surface Erosion Control

Jute mesh, plastic, geotextiles or any other sheet form of erosion control must be securely anchored at the top so it does not creep down the slope with the flow of water. Dig a trench just about a foot deep and as wide, and excavate the soil. Lay the sheeting down in the trench so there is at least 12 inches left over on the upper side of the trench. Then replace the excavated soil on top of the sheeting and tamp it down firmly. You can buy special metal anchor staples or pins, although they can be made in a pinch from heavy gauge wire coat hangers. Note: although plastic sheeting is shown on this diagram, it should not be used except in emergency where no straw, seed, or jute mesh is applied.

Unless the straw is anchored it will not remain in place for long. If the soil is moist, the straw can be forced or "punched" into the soil, which later hardens as it dries to retain the straw. Small areas can be punched with a shovel by simply pushing the blade down into the earth so many of the straw ends stand upright. Cover the entire slope this way. If the soil is soft enough, just walking back and forth on the straw with stiff boots will suffice.

To further anchor straw mulch upon very steep slopes or those subjected to wind or excessive runoff, lay a secondary covering of matting over the top. You can use jute mesh pegged down securely at regular intervals and around the edges. It will eventually decompose so you need not remove it later on. Other commercial products such as plastic netting, wood excelsior, or even chicken wire will also suffice.

JUTE MESH This widely available netting is made of jute, the organic component in many coarse ropes. To be effective it should be laid upon a seeded slope covered with a mulch layer of straw, peat, wood shavings, wood chips or hydromulch. It is sometimes used without the mulch but is much less effective that way. Special U-shaped anchor pins may be purchased to hold the edges and at intervals down the middle of each panel. Secure the top edge held by an anchor trench (see diagram). Undyed jute is completely organic in origin and will eventually decompose.

WOOD EXCELSIOR MATTING Similar to jute netting, excelsior matting is more difficult to work with and does not hold up nearly as well as jute. Use only if jute is not available. It may be laid out without mulch underneath but only if the matting is in multiple layers to one and a half inches thick. If mulch is in place beneath, thickness need be only half an inch. Excelsior matting is biodegradable and applied as per jute netting above.

GEOTEXTILES There are many new products called geotextiles that have proven to be excellent erosion control materials for difficult slopes. They are woven of space-age fibers and do not readily decompose, thus providing more-long term slope stabilization. But like any product they have benefits and problems, such as high cost factors. Before investing in a new geotextile product, consult with a civil engineer or other expert to be sure it is the most effective solution to your erosion control problems.

STRAW BALE DIKES In the wake of forest fires in the West, lines of straw bales were placed against the slopes to prevent sedimentation from filling creeks, rivers, and roadways. They act like giant brushes filtering sediment out of the moving water and slowing its descent down the canyon walls. Wire-bound bales are valuable as temporary measures in drainage ditches, canyons, swales and areas where volumes of water and accumulations of silt are expected to be concentrated. The bales are arranged nose-to-tail in a row perpendicular to the expected flow of water. Anchor each end of every bale with a 2 x 2 wood stake or #3 rebar (concrete reinforcement bar) pounded through the bale to at least 18 inches into the soil. Dikes are more effective if the bottom portion of your bales are buried about 4 inches into the soil. When immediate danger of siltation is past, bales may be taken apart and used as mulch.

SEEDING FOR EROSION CONTROL

Seeding burned or newly graded slopes with erosion control grasses and clovers is the most reliable and inexpensive means of stabilizing soil. The down side is that plants take time to germinate, then develop crowns and root systems large enough to hold back surface erosion. But seeding is the only realistic way to deal with the erosion potential of large areas of newly burned soils.

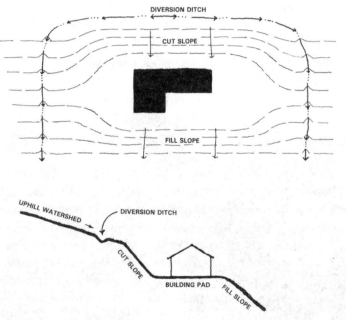

Diversion Ditches on Cut-and-Fill
The most common application of diversion ditches is along the top of cut slopes of cut-and-fill building pads. When planning a diversion ditch, remember that water flows downhill perpendicular to the slope. Visualize how water is to flow before digging in order to be sure placement of the ditch assures its effectiveness.

FIRESCAPING TIP

Diversion ditches are very effective small trenches that can channel water away from critical areas. Often water runs across many acres of watershed before it flows down onto a site. Rather than allowing the site to take the brunt of this accumulated runoff, a diversion ditch can be dug perpendicular to the slope to pick up water, direct it to the side and then down one or both edges of the incline. Diversion ditches may be used for both small- and large-scale applications and are simple to dig by hand. Always put the spoils on the downhill side of the ditch for greater strength. Larger concrete lined diversion ditches can be installed to permanently divert off-site or accumulated runoff around sensitive areas in hillside subdivisions.

In the hollows of this slope, long straw-bale siltation dikes have been laid out perpendicular to the flow of water. This not only slows down water velocity, but also captures silt and holds it, so the roadway below is not inundated. Silt is also a threat to fish and other wildlife dependent on clear water streams for survival.

There are many companies which offer their own specialized blend of seed for emergency erosion control, but they all have one species in common: annual ryegrass. Under ideal conditions annual ryegrass germinates in just a few days after sowing, which provides the most immediate plant cover crop possible. Ryegrass is also a cool season grass and will germinate under lower temperatures of winter or early spring following fire season. Annual rye grows fast and will quickly cover the slope, which buys more time for slower, more deeply rooted grasses such as fescues in the seed mix to become established. **Annual ryegrass is just that, an annual, and should not be considered a permanent solution for erosion control. It is simply the first phase of a more complex erosion control firescaping plan.**

Annual Grasses and Clover Used in Erosion Control Mixes

Bromus mollis	Blando Brome
Lolium multiflorum	Annual Ryegrass
Lolium rigidum	Wimmera-62 Ryegrass
Trifolium hirtum	Hykon Rose Clover
Trifolium subterraneum	Sub Clover
Vulpia myuros	Zorro Annual Fescue

FIRESCAPING TIP

All erosion control seed mixes have a designated application rate expressed as pounds of seed per 1,000 square feet or per acre. To order sufficient seed for your project, measure the areas as best you can and then figure how many pounds of seed is required to cover the area. If in doubt, it's better to risk applying too much seed than not enough. Thin or irregular seed distribution may leave areas vulnerable and without sufficient coverage. In general, application roles for erosion control seed mixes range from .2 to 2.0 pounds per 100 square feet, or from about 5 to 25 pounds per acre. 1 acre = 43,560 square feet.

Annual erosion control seed mixes are made up of plants that germinate quickly from seed, then mature and die off at the end of the season. With regular mowing or grazing under irrigation, their growing season may be extended slightly but this does not make them perennial. Some varieties may naturally reseed themselves and new plants can sprout each year, but there will be a dormant period which extends through the dry season until winter or spring rains, and in cold areas snow runoff to stimulate new seedlings. Therefore, annual erosion control seed mixes are temporary measures.

Perennial Plants in Erosion Control Seed Mixes

Agropyron trichlphorum	Pubescent Wheatgrass
Dactylia glomerata	Orchardgrass
Poa ampla	Sherman Big Bluegrass
Trifolium fragiferum	Strawberry Clover
Trifolium hirtum	Rose Clover
Trifolium repens	Ladino Clover

Erosion control seed mixes with perennial plants must be irrigated in arid regions to survive year 'round. Many seed mixes include both fast-germinating annuals as well as perennial plants that remain as permanent erosion control plants after the annuals die out. These include very deep rooting perennial grasses, which send out a vast network of fibrous roots to bind the soil at lower levels. Roots can eventually grow up to three feet deep with some species. Plants develop very large dumps over time, much like the buffalo sod of the Midwestern prairie.

Clovers make up a second group of essential erosion control perennials. These are nitrogen-fixing legumes which will germinate and grow even where nitrogen levels in the soil have been reduced by fire intensity. A bonus of attractive flowers appear if left unmowed, and plants bloom off and on between mowings if well irrigated. Clovers must be watered on a regular basis to live year 'round in dry climates.

IRRIGATION

This is an important factor in any erosion control or revegetation plan. If the plants are not irrigated, they must be able to survive on the average rainfall in your area, and in most cases this will limit you to annual plant species. However there are a few exceptions, such as drought-tolerant perennials which naturally die back over the summer months,

FIRESCAPING TIP

1. Some erosion control seed mixes may include the ornamental fountain grass (Pennisetum setaceum or P. ruppelii). It is added to improve the visual quality of the seeded area, but fountain grass is a highly flammable perennial grass and is listed as a species unacceptable for firescaping. Inspect the list of species on a seed mix before you buy to be sure it does not include fountain grass.
2. It is a simple matter to incorporate wildflowers into your erosion control seed, and some mixes are prepared with the flower seed already included. Where sites are irrigated, seed of other low-growing ornamental flowers can also become part of the revegetation plan. The added color is always welcome on fire-damaged sites or where new grading has disfigured the land. For largescale projects hire a landscape contractor lo help select a seed company lo design a specialized mixture for your site. The contractor will know how to set criteria that conforms to your specific irrigation, climate, and soil requirements. This service is too expensive for smaller scale projects, but there are many standard mixes which include erosion control plants, low growing wildflowers and even attractive groundcover plants. Here are a few examples of wildflowers found in these mixes:

Castilleja chromoso—Indian Paintbrush
Eschscholzio califomico—California Poppy
Gazania hybrida—Clump Gazonia
Lupinus nanus—Sky lupine
Nemophila mensiesii—Baby Blue Eyes

then resprout with the rains. These must be mowed or grazed during the summer to lower fuel volumes created by the dry leaves, seed heads, and resulting chaff. If mowed or cut with a string trimmer, the clippings must be gathered up and removed.

Irrigated sites provide more opportunities for attractive landscapes. Perennial grasses, clovers, and a variety of herbaceous groundcovers will all remain green year 'round and many flower profusely. If the plants become too tall, the stand may require a single annual mowing. On steep slopes a string trimmer may be necessary. In warm climates this is best done in the fall so the winter rains will encourage new lush growth. Further north mow at the end of winter to remove frost damage and encourage a new flush of sprouts and flowers. Creeping shrubs from the fire-resistant lists can also be spotted into this type of landscape.

PLANTING EROSION CONTROL SEED

There is a time element which influences how erosion control seed mixes are planted on newly burned sites. You can find out how and when planting occurs in your region from the Soil Conservation Service, local forestry agencies, or university extension office. The goal is to have the seed firmly in place and well germinated before heavy rains or snowfall. Unirrigated sites ideally should have light rains at first to speed germination so that when heavy rain falls it will not wash out the seed or cause serious erosion. But there is such a wide variation in weather conditions nationwide that hard and fast rules concerning planting dates are unreliable. This uncertainty is why those who expect serious erosion problems immediately after a fire often resort to mechanical methods such as plastic sheeting, netting, and geotextiles because a planting program is risky.

For smaller sites, broadcasting by hand is the best way to distribute seed, especially if straw or other organic matter and/or netting will be used. Seed remains in place better where the surface of the soil is not smooth but scarred into nooks and crannies where seed may lodge. Seed can also be distributed with a belly spreader or lawn fertilizer spreader depending on topography. Remember that seed tends to travel downward with water, so it's a good idea to sow seed more densely at the top of the slope than at the bottom. Once the seed is distributed you can lay out the mulch and netting.

HYDROSEEDING

For jobs of any size or on inaccessible slopes the hydroseed method has proven highly successful. You may have seen it in use along highways where tank trunks spray a solution of fiber, seed, water, and dye onto embankments. This method automatically covers the seed as it is applied and the dye serves to show where and how dense the slurry is sprayed. Dyes are vegetable and soon disappear. Although more expensive than doing the job by hand, hydroseeding can increase germination rates considerably. It also ensures far more even coverage, and the fibers help resist seed disturbance from sprinklers or rain.

There is a special organic glue called a tackifier which sticks the seed and mulch to very steep slopes where washout is expected. It is mixed into the tank with hydroseed mulch and seed, then sprayed directly upon the slopes. The additional cost of tackifier is a good investment because it helps to discourage seed from rolling down to the bottom of the hill.

COMBINING EROSION CONTROL SEED MIXES WITH CONTAINER PLANTS

The most successful erosion control plantings on cut-and-fill slopes includes both hydroseeding and container grown plants. Plants can be creeping shrubs from our fire-resistant plant groups or other species that have a low-growing, minimal fuel volume. The creeping shrubs should be planted first so you won't be walking over the seed or hydroseeding. Plant shrubs and trees in little niches or benches made in the slope. Once these plants are in place, seed can be hydroseeded or broadcast right over the top of them without any damage.

REVEGETATION OF NATURAL ECOSYSTEMS WITH NATIVE SPECIES

In rural communities many people own far more land than is required for the firescaping zones. After vast areas of grasses, brushland, or forests burn, both the landowners and government agencies must face the need

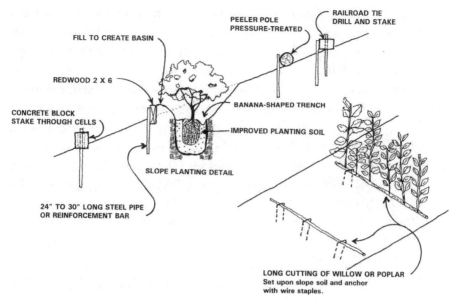

SLOPE PLANTING DETAIL

LONG CUTTING OF WILLOW OR POPLAR
Set upon slope soil and anchor
with wire staples.

Planting Shrubs and Trees on Slopes

There are many ways to create small pads on slopes where shrubs and trees can be planted. Retaining devices shown here are not absolutely necessary, but they are very helpful in preventing your pad from eroding. Willow and poplar are two types of easy-to-obtain "wattle" that can be anchored to a slope and will root if given sufficient water. Ideally this should be done in winter while cuttings are leafless, and for greater success these water-loving plants should be well irrigated. Instead of a single cutting, you can bundle up a number of them into a larger barrier that has more immediate effects on reducing runoff velocity and siltation.

for immediate revegetation. If not attended to, our waterways may be seriously affected as silt carried in the winter runoff fills up creeks and rivers to alter wildlife habitat even further.

Revegetation on a large scale is a touchy subject in some ways because there are those who feel only native species of grass should be reintroduced to the wildlands. The problem is there are few if any ecosystems comprised exclusively of native grasses because widespread grazing of livestock has spread aggressive exotic grasses and weeds from coast to coast. The notion that we can replant with native grasses to recreate a lost ecosystem is unrealistic, because runoff, wildlife, wind, and other factors will inevitably reintroduce the exotics.

Many of the grasses and clovers mentioned above are not native, yet they provide the best means of reducing erosion. When combined with native perennials, trees, and shrubs they feed wildlife and support a reasonably diverse habitat. Seed and container plants are available from commercial growers, but container-grown natives will not take on the same durable characteristics as those grown from seed sown directly into soil. To encourage native species to repopulate a burned area, gather seed from nearby unburned vegetation and sow on the burned sites. This is particularly valuable because the closer to your site the seed is gathered, the better adapted it will be to your immediate microclimate.

The forestry agency in your state can help you obtain seedling trees grown for reforestation of burned or logged forest lands. These are small, only about 12 inches tall. The bare-root plants, both deciduous and evergreen, are least expensive and available only during the winter or very early spring. Container-grown stock can be planted any time of year. There are two sizes available in long, thin containers which look like milk cartons. The larger ones are 40-cubic-inch containers and the smaller measure only 13 cubic inches.

Special plastic net sleeves and bamboo anchor stakes can be obtained which protect each seedling from foraging animals and foot traffic. The plastic sleeve is made of photo-degradable material that eventually decomposes from exposure to sunlight after the seedling matures. The little trees are easy to step on while planting and afterward if not marked with these devices.

Replanting native oak trees is a simple matter of collecting the acorns from local healthy and sprouting them. Oaks have long tap roots which help the young plants survive the dryness of their first summer by tapping moisture deep in the soil. This is why they do not grow well in containers and after transplanting the mortality rate is extremely high. Landscape architects and foresters struggled with their oak plantings for years, testing this container and that, various planting seasons and watering, but still the success rate was barely 50 percent. Those that managed to survive failed to thrive. Studies eventually showed that acorns planted just after

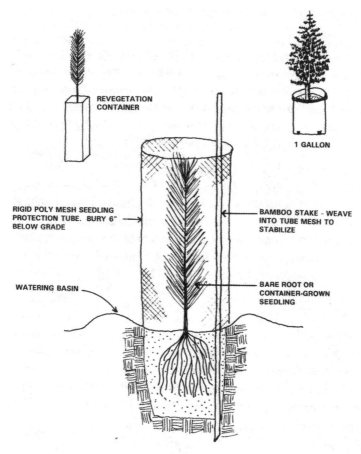

REVEGETATION CONTAINER

1 GALLON

RIGID POLY MESH SEEDLING PROTECTION TUBE. BURY 6" BELOW GRADE

BAMBOO STAKE - WEAVE INTO TUBE MESH TO STABILIZE

WATERING BASIN

BARE ROOT OR CONTAINER-GROWN SEEDLING

Commercially Grown Revegetation Tree Planting

Whether you plant five seedlings or five hundred, they should all be protected with the mesh protection tube to prevent rabbits and other wildlife from feeding on the succulent little trees. It helps to bury the net into the planting hole a few inches to discourage burrowing animals, but this may prove difficult. The bamboo stakes—up to 36 inches long—help you know where each free is located. Contact your state forestry agency for growers and suppliers near you.

they crack open to sprout have an 80- to 90-percent success rate. Today revegetation nurseries grow and sell "cracked" or "sprouted" acorns at certain times of year.

You can either plant acorns or ensure their viability by sprouting them before planting. Either way gather the acorns in the fall and discard any which show discoloration or maggot holes. Then place them in the refrigerator for a month, or if you live in a cold climate simply store them outdoors. Then plant as indicated below. To sprout acorns and similar nut trees first set the acorns in a container of moist rooting medium such as sand, perlite, or vermiculite and keep moist. Those which are viable will crack slightly within about six weeks and the tip of the root becomes visible. That is the time to plant them from two to six inches deep in native soil. Bulb planting tools are perfect for this! In forests and brushland, acorns lying on top of the soil can be found sprouted and the tap root already extending well into the soil. This proves some species of native oaks are not too particular about planting depth. It helps to use the netting or a stake to mark where each acorn is planted to avoid stepping on them and compacting the soil above the developing stem. Plant extras to allow for natural mortality losses.

To reforest or revegetate extensive areas after burns with native plants, it's a good idea to consult with a professional forester, botanist, or landscape architect before you begin. Their experience and advice will help ensure your efforts are successful. Wildlife biologists are also very helpful in reestablishing habitat to encourage regeneration of wildlife in burned areas.

10

TIPS FOR FIRE-SAFE HOMESITES

omes are burned down by wildland fires that originate outside the house or a house fire that begins inside. A house fire close to wildlands can ignite a raging forest fire, and every homeowner should realize that there is a perpetual risk of this happening with increasing urban-wildland interface. Should you or your homesite be the source of a wildfire in some states, you will be held financially responsible for the costs incurred fighting the blaze and for other damage it causes. In some communities laws mandate creation of defensible space around every homesite. This makes keeping a fire-safe homesite not just an option, but a necessity, for the legal and financial ramifications are awesome indeed.

FIRE-SAFE MAINTENANCE

POWER LINES Electrical lines supplying power to a house or connecting outbuildings often pass through tree canopies, and in some cases are actually attached to trees instead of poles. Branches rubbing against wires or those dose enough to make contact in windy weather are potential hazards. The friction over time will wear down the insulation and ignite the tree. If you see a problem, alert the utility company, since it may be their responsibility to trim back vegetation. Cut back all tree branches so there are no contacts with the wire, or reroute your wiring so it bypasses the trees. Electrical lines improperly installed connecting outbuildings can also be a serious hazard.

FIRE WOOD OR SCRAP LUMBER These accumulations of fuel should be stacked at least 30 feet from the house. Most people don't comply because they find it inconvenient to carry their cordwood that far, especially in the snow. If there is a wildfire, however, these fuel stacks become a haven for embers, which will ignite sooner or later, and when in contact with the house it is sure to burn as well.

PROPANE GAS TANK Propane tanks are extremely explosive and become a serious threat to firefighters in any kind of fire. Locate propane tanks no closer than 30 feet from the house for safety. Keep a radius of 10 feet on all sides clear of flammable debris and vegetation. Remember: propane is heavier than air and tends to pool at ground level.

ACCESS Be sure firefighters can find your home quickly. Roads should be clearly marked and your house displayed with large street numbers along with your name if possible. Keep driveways and private roads free of encroaching vegetation and provide turnouts at regular intervals. Get together with your neighbors so their homes are similarly marked to speed response time for any emergency. Often firefighters are brought in from out of state on big burns and are not familiar with the local community. They rely strictly on maps, which in turn are based on street names and house numbers. If any one of these are absent, rescue workers may be delayed or never find your house at all. In addition, house numbers are an important aspect of reckoning, and without them drivers may get lost.

FUEL ACCUMULATIONS Homesites should be kept free of brush piles, accumulations of leaves, garbage, glass, oily rags, and other combustible fuels that may feed a fire. Never use gasoline as a cleaning agent.

CHIMNEY OR STOVE PIPE Sparks rising with smoke from indoor fires is a serious hazard. Cap chimneys and stove pipes with an approved spark arrestor. Keep tree branches pruned at least 15 feet back from the chimney.

DECKS Outdoor wood decking can pose a significant hazard if fuels are allowed to accumulate in the space beneath them. Do not store firewood beneath your deck. Keep all weeds removed with an annual application of herbicide and screen it off or finish with siding.

SAFE RURAL BURNING

In many rural communities people burn household and garden refuse outdoors. Wildfires are frequently started by these outdoor bonfires, and the risk of burning should be weighed against other methods of waste disposal. However, where there is no garbage pickup, burning is the only realistic method of disposing of combustible materials. Despite disadvantages to air quality, there are a few instances when agricultural burning is the only way to deal with large accumulations of slash due to land clearing. It is always better to safely burn slash than to leave it piled up indefinitely as a potential fuel pocket for wildfires.

Every state, county, and city has its own rules about outdoor debris burning. These can vary considerably, so do not use hearsay information. For example, the Denver area has such strict burning regulations that indoor fires from a fireplace or wood stove are absolutely forbidden on certain days. Find out directly from the county yourself because you may be required to file a burn permit. **Always read the entire permit to verify if there are any designated restrictions. Call your local agency that issued the permit before *each* day you intend to burn in order to find out if it is still valid.** Under certain hazardous conditions permits may be rescinded without notice, and it's up to you to find out.

It doesn't take laws or permits to exercise common sense. If you have a permit and insist on burning during improper weather and a wildfire results, you are liable. Permits are not carte blanche to burn indiscriminately. Don't burn on windy days or when it is very hot and dry. Burning when there is a threat of rain during the winter ensures any lingering coals will be doused with rainfall. Don't let children, pets, or livestock have access to burning areas. **Do not illegally burn at night to avoid detection.**

There are two ways outdoor burning is done. A **burn barrel** is usually an open-topped, 50-gallon drum. It must be fully intact and made of heavy-gauge steel to retain the flames, and tall enough to prevent the material inside from spilling over. The top should be covered with a small mesh (one-fourth inch min), heavy-gauge screen so embers are not allowed to rise up and out of the barrel. There should be at least 10 feet cleared of any combustible materials on all sides of the barrel. Never put aerosol cans, toxic substances, or containers of flammable materials inside a burn barrel. If permits are required, you must have a valid burn permit to incinerate trash in a burn barrel. When the fire burns out, do not dump the ash out in an exposed pile. Dig a hole, pour the ashes into it and wet the mass down, then cover it up again.

FIRESCAPING TIP

If you have had your land cleared by heavy equipment, or are aware of poison oak, sumac, or poison ivy in a burn pile, be very cautious. Oils from the roots, trunk, branches, leaves, berries, and flowers are all toxic and will travel in the smoke if burned. Reactions can occur in the mouth, throat, and lungs if the smoke is inhaled, and the eyes may also be affected. If there is a possibility of poison oak in your burn pile, wear a respirator, eye protection, or better yet, don't burn it. For many, contact with burn pile smoke has become a life-threatening experience.

Poison oak. This native plant is widespread throughout the West. Its characteristic three-leaf pattern is easy to recognize, but in winter it is leafless—though no less toxic. Poison oak leafs out in the spring, then develops a reddish tinge in late summer and fall.

Open fires are a popular way to burn garden refuse such as prunings, leaves, tree stumps, and brush. They are piled up over many months or all at once with heavy equipment. One mistake frequently made is trying to burn too large a pile at once, because accumulations of dry brush and tree limbs can fuel an incredibly hot fire. Trying to douse one of these with a garden hose is like spitting into a fireplace. It is better to create a smaller fire near the pile and gradually feed material into it in a controlled fashion. **The fire should be no more than 4 feet in diameter at any time.**

Burn piles should never be placed near forests, buildings, fields, or dry grass. Clear the ground completely before starting to burn and be sure there is at least ten feet clear on all sides of the fire. A water supply must be dose at hand, with a shovel and bucket. Although it is a common occurrence in rural areas, **do not leave the fire unattended**, even if it is just a smoldering pile of ash. Make sure it is completely extinguished by wetting the ash before you leave.

11

GETTING HELP: PUBLIC AGENCIES AND PRIVATE PROFESSIONALS

The majority of this book deals with issues of concern before a wildfire strikes. It is a preventative approach designed to help every homeowner in rural areas and those within the urban-wildfire interface. Unfortunately, protective measures of establishing defensible space and installation of an emergency water supply are rarely attended to. As a result many readers today may be faced with the task of rebuilding a burn-out homesite.

In most states there is a network of agricultural, horticultural, and landscape industry professionals who offer assistance with revegetation or improving fire resistance of homesites. In many cases the services are free of charge, but professionals such as landscape architects and civil engineers are well worth their fees in designing attractive yet highly functional firescapes.

PUBLIC AGENCIES

During these times of tight fiscal constraints within all levels of government, there will be continual changes in the names, scope of work, and services offered by public agencies. Some may disappear altogether. But while they still exist you may take advantage of a wide variety of inexpensive or free literature and benefit from the professionals on staff.

USDA Natural Resources Conservation Service (www.nrcs.usda .gov) This federal agency is the most valuable for obtaining government assistance or guidance in implementing any of the land management concepts important before and after wildfire. Their offices are scattered throughout the United States but more commonly in rural areas. Experts in agronomy and civil engineering, their field agents will help to determine soil type, water holding capacity, and vegetation management. They can be of service for the construction of safe and retentive ponds or reservoirs. Large-scale disturbance of vegetation may result in siltation, slope destabilization, and increased runoff somewhere else. This agency helps to identify and mitigate all these potential problems before you begin work.

USDA US Forest Service (www.fs.fed.us) The Forest Service is concerned with wildfire in national forests. This is an excellent wildfire resource as well as extensive resources for land management. They are geared to assist professionals and other agencies in their local fire and forestry efforts.

STATE FORESTRY AGENCIES The best place to find up-to-date information and advice on local conditions is at your state department of forestry. Fire protection is a very local issue and this is the jumping off point for the most useful and up to date information for where you live. This includes degree of wildfire risk, ecosystems, and many weather with other factors that vary considerably from state to state. They provide programs to help residents create more defensible homesites and increase awareness of fire danger. State forestry staff will tell you where the forest tree nurseries are located and how to obtain trees for replanting burned areas.

US FISH AND WILDLIFE SERVICE (USFWS) This is the the agency that can be helpful when seeking information regarding wildlife habitat on or around your land. They can tell you how these wildlife protection regulations may ultimately influence wildfire vulnerability of existing residences and proposed new homesites.

STATE FISH AND GAME AGENCIES The state agency concerned with wildlife management Agents may be willing to make a site visit to assist in any wildlife-related aspects of firescape development before wildfire and revegetation afterward.

LOCAL FIRE STATION Many suburban areas are served by municipal fire departments which have experts available to help with fire prevention and development of firescapes. They also offer fire prevention literature and may make a site visit to your home to discuss ways to make it less vulnerable to fire.

UNIVERSITY COOPERATIVE EXTENSION SERVICE   There is an excellent network of information and assistance which ties local agriculture to university systems. Often labeled as "Farm Advisor" for any particular county. This is also the origin of Master Gadener programs to help you select plants for revegetation. A Master Gardener can make a site visit to diagnose serious issues such as plant diseases in firescapes.

CITY OR COUNTY PUBLIC WORKS OR PLANNING DEPARTMENTS   In many fire-prone counties there are strict codes as to what is allowable in terms of vegetation management on a piece of property. Some private communities require permission from homeowner's associations to remove trees or even native shrubs. It is important to discuss with your local planning department any large scale vegetation adjustments for firescapes. This goes for reservoir and pond construction as well.

PRIVATE PROFESSIONALS

Private sector experts can be hired for an hourly fee to design a firescape and emergency water system. More and more private wildfire consultants are popping up in the Western states who link new products and technologies with consumer homesite needs. These experts are not usually bound by the limitations of government employees in terms of services provided, so long as you are willing to pay the fees. It's important to know that in recent years there has been a dramatic rise in fee schedules for these professionals due to more stringent licensing requirements and the costs of litigation. You can expect to pay from $50 to $150 per hour for any one of them. Licensing, titles and other regulations vary considerably from state to state. **It's always a good idea to verify the status of a professional's license before signing a contract.**

ARCHITECT   A licensed architect will be informed as to the fire resistance of various building materials and should also be able to design a home with cutting-edge fireproof qualities. An architect can also help you replace certain features of an existing home to make it less vulnerable to fire.

LANDSCAPE ARCHITECT   A landscape architect is the best person to help you with firescaping, but in some states there is no licensing of these professionals. Where licensing is required, inquire whether or not he or she has experience in this field, otherwise you're on your own. These professionals will help you to combine fire-resistant plants along with other materials into an attractive landscape.

CIVIL ENGINEER   For design of emergency water supply and a delivery system, a licensed civil engineer is the best choice for calculating the proper fire water flows. Often an older, partially retired engineer who retains a valid license can be more economically hired to develop systems than a full-time engineer with a busy practice. Because the water storage and delivery can be expensive to install and must function perfectly, it is best to have it professionally designed to avoid any problems down the road. Engineers are also invaluable in issues of slope stabilization, design of retaining walls, and installation of extensive drainage devices.

LANDSCAPE CONTRACTOR   If you aren't going to plant your own firescape, a licensed landscape contractor may be able to design an attractive planting plan using plants and concepts detailed in this book. There should be a plan prepared ahead of time showing how the planting will look, then an installation cost prepared. This professional can also design and install an irrigation system for the firescape as well.

FORESTER OR REGISTERED ARBORIST   These are experts who deal exclusively in trees and should be consulted before any large-scale tree removal is done. They can help evaluate the health of every tree and provide guidance as to which individuals or species should be either preserved or removed. Other factors, such as longevity, wind loading, and structural form, will influence the safest, most successful forest and tree management. Foresters can assist if selective logging is required to thin out overcrowded forests on larger scale properties. These professionals should be members of either the American Forestry Association, American Society of Consulting Arborists, International Society of Arboriculture, or the National Arborist Association.

TREE SERVICE   The tree service industry is not well regulated so you can be vulnerable to unscrupulous operators or considerable liability if something goes wrong. Ask for references, proof of insurance, contractor's license, and verify all of these before hiring. Those companies owned by arborists or foresters are more likely to do a sensitive job. For large jobs, consult a second company for a comparative estimate just as you would seek more than one medical opinion before submitting to surgery. Be sure to discuss costs of clean up and hauling.

EMOTIONAL SUPPORT

For those who have experienced a wildfire firsthand, the faintest whiff of smoke in the air will kindle instant panic. People who have lost their homes may never overcome the fear of fire. Others who may not be close to fires but see the devastation on the evening news may grow just as paranoid as the actual victims. Fear of wildfires is nothing to scoff at and should be treated as other overwhelming phobias by a trained professional. If left untreated the fear may grow to unmanageable proportions and become difficult to live with.

Mental health professionals tell us that those who have lost a home to fire feel the same kind of grieving as they would for a deceased loved one. The memories, possessions, household pets, even the sense of self can be destroyed with one's place of residence. To rebuild may seem an insurmountable task even if there are sufficient funds from insurance.

Unlike an isolated housefire, whole communities can be devastated by wildfires which leaves many with nowhere to live and no place to go home to. Some burned-out neighborhoods perish entirely. It is likely there will be mental health professionals available to fire victims and therapy groups organized. Contact local mental health organizations for news on new groups.

The trauma of wildfire may also be eased by a private counselor or psychiatrist. These professionals can assist over the long-term with easing the losses and the fear of recurring fires. Many HMOs will cover part or all the costs of this type of counseling.

RESOURCES

OBTAINING PLANTS

Obtaining the plants listed in this book should not be difficult as most, if not all, are readily available in the nursery trade. If the local nursery or garden center doesn't have some in stock, it's not difficult to special order them for you. Problems arise most often in rural areas, which may not enjoy a thriving retail nursery trade.

SEED SOURCES FOR EROSION CONTROL AND IRRIGATED PASTURE*

Bulk seed for revegetation and erosion control is widely available from local agricultural suppliers, feed stores, and retail nurseries. Buying directly from a local supplier will save you shipping charges, particularly for large, heavy orders. Wildflowers are sold either as individual species or predesigned mixes. They are the best place to find a wide variety to choose from with seed more economically priced in bulk, by the pound.

Applewood Seed Co.
www.applewoodseed.com
Wildflower seed mixes for a wide range of climates nationwide.

Clyde Robin Seed Company
www.clyderobin.com
Able to handle large bulk orders for revegetation or mowable grasslands.

Ernst Seeds
www.ernstseed.com
Hard core conservation seed mixes for restoring sites after mining and landfills. Specific climate blends are valueable for mountain areas.

Granite Seed and Erosion Control
https://graniteseed.com
Wide range of native and site adapted plants for revegetation and supplies for erosion control.

Peaceful Valley Farm Supply
www.groworganic.com
Ideal for community level erosion control projects with agricultural approach to revegetation for livestock.

*Sources were viable at the time this book was written. The author is not responsible for discontinued companies or changes of address.

INDEX